Revd Dr Mark Stibbe has, since September 1996, been the Senior Leader of St Andrew's Church Chorleywood, a large Charismatic Anglican Church just outside London. He is a best-selling and prolific author as well as a preacher much in demand both in the UK and overseas. He has travelled extensively in the UK, Europe, Australasia and the United States. He employs an approach that combines both the Word and the Spirit, and has seen God move in wonderful ways over the years. He is married to Alie, who is also a writer, and has four children aged between eight and sixteen – Philip, Hannah, Johnathan and Sam. In his spare time he likes to play cricket, watch movies, or eat out.

DRAWING NEAR TO GOD

The Temple Model of Prayer

MARK STIBBE

Foreword by Canon Andrew White

DARTON·LONGMAN+TODD

Published in 2005 by
Darton, Longman and Todd Ltd
1 Spencer Court
140–142 Wandsworth High Street
London SW18 4JJ

First published as *A Kingdom of Priests* in 1994
by Darton, Longman and Todd Ltd

ISBN 0-232-52582-X

A catalogue record for this book is available from the British Library.

Designed by Sandie Boccacci
Phototypeset in 11/13pt Ehrhardt by Intype Libra Ltd
Printed and bound in Great Britain by
CPI Bath, Bath

To my wife Alie

CONTENTS

FOREWORD

The Temple Model of Prayer

As I write I look at the walls of Jerusalem: the place of the Holy Temple of the Lord. The Rabbis say that Jerusalem is where heaven and earth meet, and if there is a precise spot where this has happened in history it must be on Mount Moriah, the Holy Mountain where the Temple once stood. It was in the Temple that the Shekinah glory of God resided, it was here that the priests and people would meet with God.

Mark Stibbe's book on 'The Temple Model of Prayer' takes the reader into that Holy Place where heaven and earth meet. No longer do you physically need to be here in Jerusalem. By practising this Temple model of prayer a way is made available for us to enter into that same intimacy with God that once only the High Priest could experience.

This is not just another Christian paperback. *Drawing Near to God* is a powerful and beautiful tool which will enable every follower of Jesus to enter into a new depth of relationship with Him and our Father through the power of the Holy Spirit. It opens the gates of heaven so that we also can be in that place where heaven and earth meet. Stibbe's book is written with great historical, biblical and theological accuracy, and redresses theology's neglect of the Priestly Covenant in a way that is both practical and approachable.

Living mainly between Jerusalem and Baghdad I am painfully aware of the broken nature of our world. In a world of brokenness and suffering we all need occasional glimpses of the glory of heaven. This book enables that to happen, as the reader is taken on a journey to the glory of the throne room of God. If ever a tool like this was needed it is now. An exceptional book like almost no other lies at your fingertips. Read it, go on a journey to the Glory of God, and your prayer life will be changed forever.

CANON ANDREW WHITE
Jerusalem, All Saints Day 2004

AUTHOR'S PREFACE

It is a real joy to be able to produce a new, fully revised edition of what was originally called *A Kingdom of Priests*. First published in 1994, many people have told me how it helped them to grow in personal prayer. It has humbled me to receive letters from people sharing how God has spoken to them through the book, breathing the fresh air of his Spirit into their devotional lives. When it went out of print a few years ago, I was astonished by how often I was asked for this book. Letters have come from many and varied locations asking if I have any spare copies. It seems that the Temple model of prayer described in these pages has struck a chord deep in the hearts of many believers. Even this morning, as I sat at my desk preparing to write this preface to the new edition, a letter arrived from a lady called Joan. This is quite typical of what I have received over recent years, from people of all ages:

> Dear Revd Stibbe
> I write to thank you for your book *A Kingdom of Priests (Deeper into God in Prayer)*. I found it in a second-hand bookshop and read it, and I have been greatly blessed. I am 81 and have been a Christian since a student at college, but these lessons from the Temple have opened a whole new dimension of prayer. I would love to share it with others, particularly with some of my praying friends . . . If you have a spare copy, I'd be grateful if you could post it to me.

It is because of the many people like Joan who have asked for copies of *A Kingdom of Priests* that I am thrilled that Darton, Longman and Todd have agreed this year (ten years since the first edition) to the publishing of a brand new version.

Not only have individuals found the Temple model helpful, whole churches have as well. A friend of mine, Revd Anne Douglas, was vicar of a church in an urban priority area. During that time she and her congregation completely rebuilt their church. Having read *A Kingdom of Priests*, they used the Temple model as their inspiration. Anne takes up the story:

> To come up with a design for a new church is an exciting prospect. When that has to also function as a multi-purpose building, open seven days a week to serve a deprived community, yet also be recognisable as a place of worship, glorifying Almighty God, we wanted to give Him the best we could, with a very limited budget.
>
> Our first principle was an open door – for as many hours in the day as possible, and that it should be welcoming to all comers. We wanted people who came in off the street to know there was a difference, and even if they came in to 'The Hatch' for a quick lunch, or in to see an adviser who could help them get work, through the church-based charity 'ASCEND', there was to be a sense of His presence that would draw them deeper. The model of the Temple as described in *A Kingdom of Priests* was our inspiration for the new building. The concept was that the further one moved through the building, it was a prophetic demonstration of how one moved on in prayer, and in one's faith, in how we minister to God in our lives as a church.
>
> So outside, just at the entrance, is the 'living water fountain', and the main doors and porch are as imposing, yet welcoming, and in this area, we in the church frequently gave thanks here for all God was doing in the life of the church, and in this place – the 'gates of thanksgiving'. The foyer area is large, and houses the café, and also the reception area for the charity. We considered this as the 'courts of the Gentiles' – a safe place for all to come in, and it is there that many people, over a cuppa, would meet a church member, and where relationships would be built.
>
> A sound-proof but movable wall opens into the centre part of the building, with its high ceiling and clerestory windows, which is used throughout the week for parent and toddler groups, and other church-based activities, as well as being the main worship area on a Sunday – 'the courts of praise'.
>
> A further movable wall opens into the chapel, which serves as a sanctuary space for Sundays and during the week is used for prayer, small services, etc. So [this is] 'the holy place' and

here there is much laid on the 'altar of sacrifice', in the ongoing ministry of the church.

Along the sides of the building, off the corridors are various meeting rooms, classrooms, crèche etc. – all used for activities of 'growth' – in a secular sense through the courses offered to the unemployed, but also for Alpha, children's groups etc. Thus as we move through the building, so we live out our growth in faith.

Work and worship are closely entwined in the Hebrew language, and we learnt what it was to *be* the church, in the years before we had a building, so when we were to get our new church, it was important that it became a place where we could 'live out' our faith.

Anne Douglas, Vicar of All Saints Oxhey 1994–2002

It is truly thrilling to hear how the Temple model of prayer has not only restructured people's private devotions but also whole church communities. Indeed, just as thrilling has been the news that missionaries have found it helpful too. One of my most encouraging letters was from a missionary who sent me a photograph (still on my computer) of her teaching the Temple model in Africa.

So what – besides the title and the cover – is new about *Drawing Near to God: The Temple Model of Prayer?*

For a start, you will find that I have completely rewritten the Introduction. I did this because nearly 20 years of using the same method of daily prayer inevitably yields new insights and greater maturity. There would be something very wrong if it did not. So the Introduction brings out something of these fresh riches, particularly the emphasis on 'intimacy with God' implicit in the idea of 'drawing near'. If there is one area that I have been consistently developing over the last ten years of my Christian life, it would be intimacy with the Father. This journey is reflected in my book *From Orphans to Heirs*, but it is also visible in other books I have written as well as in my preaching.

In addition, I have added a new chapter on 'preparing for the journey'. The more I pray using the structure of the Temple, the more I recognise the need to be led by the Holy Spirit. Without the work of the Spirit, this model could become all form but no fire. In Chapter 1, I give some advice on preparing for the journey through the Temple courts, stressing the vital need to welcome the Holy Spirit.

Chapters 2 and 3 have been rewritten in the light of my experience over the last two decades of praying using this model. New material has been added and existing material updated. Some of the original material has been cut out where it has either felt like it interrupted the flow of the prose, or it represented a voice not yet sufficiently mature in God. I have to confess there were one or two moments when I was quite glad of the chance to rewrite the book!

Chapter 4 has been substantially rewritten in the part on intercessory prayer. I have a whole new section on the breastplate worn by Aaron and the high priests of Israel when they went into the Holy Place. They carried the names of the 12 tribes of Israel on their hearts, engraved on precious jewels. This image has inspired me in my intercessory ministry. I now use the picture of the jewel-encrusted breastplate as a vital *aide-mémoire* in prayer. I have the names and subjects of prayer written on my heart as I represent them before the Father in intercession.

This brings me to another difference between the original and this new edition. In *A Kingdom of Priests* the fifth chapter put the spotlight on beholding the throne in prayer, particularly using the discipline of praying back the Scriptures (such as Revelation 4—5). The emphasis in the original fell very much on the transcendence of God. In the rewrite I am more balanced, emphasising that the King whom we meet on the throne is also our Dad. For me the highest goal of prayer is to enter the throne-room of heaven and to spend time experiencing the Father's embrace, basking in his smile, and returning his affections with the highest praise. This, I would say, points to the most important difference between *A Kingdom of Priests* and *Drawing Near to God*. In this new edition, prayer has much more to do with a growing intimate communion with our Father in heaven. We reach the purest expression of this before the throne of God.

Chapter 7 is pretty well entirely new, as we look back at the journey described in the Temple model of prayer, describe some basic guidelines for using the model, and then point to the importance of continuing communication with the Father beyond our structured devotional time.

In addition I have extended the Appendices to include a more up-to-date example of how the Temple model of prayer can be applied in a corporate worship event.

My prayer is that *Drawing Near to God* will be used to bring personal revival to your devotional life and fresh vision for corporate worship and prayer in the local church.

MARK STIBBE
May 2004

LIST OF ILLUSTRATIONS

ACKNOWLEDGEMENTS

First and foremost, I am extremely grateful to my wife Alie for having a vision to see *A Kingdom of Priests* republished in a new, updated format. Alie directs a small business called Word and Spirit Resources Ltd, dedicated to getting my many books and tapes (and increasingly her own as well) to the widest possible number of people, both in the UK and worldwide. It was Alie who received the majority of requests for *A Kingdom of Priests* to be re-released and it was she who approached Darton, Longman and Todd with the idea of running with this again. I am so grateful to her for doing this. As I have rewritten the book, it has increased my vision and passion for the Temple model of prayer and also given me a glimpse of the road I have travelled in my own spiritual life since the first edition. So thank you to Alie and to Darton, Longman and Todd for their hard work.

Secondly, I want to acknowledge those who have influenced my thinking on worship and prayer. Some of these men and women of God are mentioned and indeed quoted in this volume. Where I have known the original source for the quotations, I have identified that in the notes at the end of the book. Where I have not had the source (we all pick up quotes over the years, and many of these do not have sources attached), I ask for the authors' indulgence in quoting them without full details. The fact is, I have been enriched by countless different writers and speakers. These influences come from many different sources, ancient and modern – Jewish, Orthodox, Catholic, Mystical, Pentecostal, and so forth. I want to express my gratitude to all my past and present teachers in the school of prayer. I sit like a small child on the shoulders of some great giants of Christian spirituality. I am truly grateful.

Introduction

The deepest cry within the human heart is the cry for intimate communion with God. The soul yearns for this re-connection in a way that it yearns for no other thing on earth. Most of us, sooner or later, look up at the stars and ask the fundamental question, 'Is there anyone out there?' 'Is there some divine person or being with whom I can enjoy an eternal friendship?' At some point or other, most people enter into a spiritual quest for something – or better still, some One – divine. A fundamental desire for God drives us to search for that which lies beyond the realms of the ordinary. We seek the most profound of reassurances. In the words of a famous rock ballad, we say, 'tell me there's a heaven'.

In January 1977 I experienced my own spiritual homecoming. After a time of deep soul-searching, I came to believe that Jesus Christ had died for my sins and that he had been raised from the dead and is alive today. On 17 January 1977, aged sixteen, I entrusted my life to the Lord Jesus and came home to the One whom Jesus called 'our Father'. A journey began that night which I am still following today. Having been reconciled to my Father in heaven through the passion of the Son of God, I have been seeking to walk in the Spirit ever since. This, more than anything else, has meant an ever-deepening intimacy of communion with the Father.

A Kingdom of Those Who Draw Near

Nearly 20 years ago I found myself sitting in a church in London. I had been a Christian for about ten years and I had started running out of enthusiasm in my prayer life. I had been employing a very simple model of prayer that had been given to me by the man who mentored me as a new Christian. This model involved the acrostic A-C-T-S, and comprised Adoration, Confession, Thanksgiving and Supplication. This had served its purpose for a time, but after ten years I was looking to move on and go deeper with God. I felt somewhat dry in prayer and needed fresh inspiration.

Sitting in the church reflecting on these things, I was suddenly reminded of the promise of God in Exodus 19:6. It is important to remember the context if we are to fully appreciate this passage. The Israelites have escaped from Egypt, have crossed the Red Sea, and are now gathered at Mount Sinai for the giving of the Law. Encamped at the foot of the mountain, the people receive the following revelation through the prophet Moses:

> Then Moses climbed the mountain to appear before God. The LORD called out to him from the mountain and said, 'Give these instructions to the descendants of Jacob, the people of Israel: "You have seen what I did to the Egyptians. You know how I brought you to myself and carried you on eagle's wings. Now if you will obey me and keep my covenant, you will be my own special treasure from among all the nations of the earth; for all the earth belongs to me. And you will be to me a kingdom of priests, my holy nation." Give this message to the Israelites.'
>
> Exodus 19:3–6

The phrase that struck me back then, and still impacts me today, is the expression 'a kingdom of priests'. God's intention right from the very beginning was to have a people that would be his special treasure. This people would have one gift above all others: an intimate relationship with the Living God. The word 'priests' in this verse is the word *kohanim* in Hebrew (*kohen* in the singular). Many Jewish people today have the surname Cohen, which is the same word. Literally, a *kohen* is someone who draws near. The phrase 'a kingdom of priests' means 'a kingdom of those who draw near to the Father'. God's promise through Moses was that his people could enjoy this friendship with himself provided they continued in obedience to him. Faithfulness would bring the reward of ever-increasing intimacy for God's people – an ever-increasing sense of their dearness to God and God's nearness to them (to use a phrase of Sarah Edwards). Disobedience would result in a sense of God's absence rather than his presence.

As I remembered this wonderful promise, my mind started to wander with God's people through all the meandering twists and turns of their journey thereafter. I remembered how they so often forgot this promise, disobeyed the Father, and found themselves living with judgement rather than favour. Ultimately this unfaithfulness resulted in God's people losing their home and their Temple. Exiled to Babylon (modern Iraq), God's people wept for Jerusalem, now in ruins, and mourned the destruction of Solomon's Temple and the loss of the Ark of the Covenant, the symbol of God's presence. But the Father, in his mercy, shared his heart through the prophets of the Exile, reassuring his people that they would return to the land and that the Messiah would one day come to reconcile them to himself. The prophet Isaiah foresaw this day when, under the inspiration of the Holy Spirit, he declared:

> The Spirit of the Sovereign LORD is upon me, because the LORD has appointed me to bring good news to the poor. He has sent me to comfort the brokenhearted and to announce that captives will be released and prisoners will be freed.
>
> Isaiah 61:1–2

The prophecy goes on to promise a restoration of that priestly intimacy promised through Moses in Exodus 19:6:

> You will be called priests of the LORD, ministers of our God. You will be fed with the treasures of the nations and will boast in their riches. Instead of shame and dishonour, you will inherit a double portion of prosperity and everlasting joy.
>
> Isaiah 61:6–7

As I meditated on this great promise, my thoughts turned to the time of Jesus. There was a great expectation in his day that the Messiah would come and fulfil the promise of Isaiah 61. After being baptised in the Holy Spirit, and warring with the devil in the desert, Jesus came to Nazareth and preached on Isaiah 61:

> When he came to the village of Nazareth, his boyhood home, he went as usual to the synagogue on the Sabbath and stood up to read the Scriptures. The scroll containing the messages of Isaiah the prophet was handed to him, and he unrolled the scroll to the place where it says:
>
> > The Spirit of the Lord is upon me,
> > for he has appointed me to preach Good News to the poor.

He has sent me to proclaim
that captives will be released,
that the blind will see,
that the downtrodden will be freed from their oppressors,
and that the time of the Lord's favour has come.

He rolled up the scroll, handed it back to the attendant, and sat down. Everyone in the synagogue stared at him intently. Then he said, 'This Scripture has come true today before your very eyes!'

Luke 4:16–21

Jesus Christ came to restore a sense of God's nearness. He came to create a kingdom of those who draw near to the Father. He did this throughout his three-year ministry as he preached about the Kingdom of God, healed the sick and set the captives free. He invited all to enter this merciful, inclusive Kingdom, however sinful. The only entry requirements were to repent and believe. Then, at the end of his life, Jesus endured what Mel Gibson has described as 'the passion of the Christ'. Through his suffering and death, Jesus Christ achieved what human beings could never have achieved through their own self-effort – reconciliation with the Father. The ultimate goal of Jesus' work was therefore 'relational' in character. Indeed, Christianity is more a relationship than a religion. It is all about intimate union with the Father, through Jesus, in the power of the Spirit. It is because of Jesus' death, resurrection and ascension, and of course the outpouring of the Spirit at Pentecost, that we can draw near to the Father. Thanks to Jesus, all people – whether Jew or Gentile – can hear and receive this truth:

You are a kingdom of priests, God's holy nation, his very own possession. This is so you can show others the goodness of God, for he called you out of the darkness into his wonderful light. 'Once you were not a people; now you are the people of God. Once you received none of God's mercy; now you have received his mercy.'

1 Peter 2:9–10

The Temple Model of Prayer

As I dwelt on these wonderful truths, I sensed the Holy Spirit impressing on me not only the privilege of this great gift but also my own individual responsibility. Prayer is relationship with the Father, simple as that. It is an act of divine–human co-operation in which I draw near to the Father, and in which the Father draws near to me. If those who follow Jesus Christ are the true inheritors of the promise of Exodus 19:6, then we are a kingdom of *kohanim*, of those who draw near. But this is not a passive enterprise, in which Christians simply sit and wait for God – intimacy by osmosis, as it were. There is an active role we have to play. Indeed, we are to take the initiative. As the brother of Jesus said, 'Draw close to God, and God will draw close to you' (James 4:8).

Put another way, if we invest time and energy in our intimacy with the Father, he will more than meet us halfway and grant us that sense of his nearness to us.

In attempting this, the A-C-T-S model had served me reasonably well for nearly ten years. But now I found myself feeling dry spiritually. It seemed to lack life, colour, depth and intimacy. Prayer is, after all, like love; it is a many-splendoured thing. It is a gem capable of many refractions. Yet for me it had become a monochrome ritual: a mechanical procedure rather than a great delight. Put briefly, I needed personal revival in prayer. I was ready for a new lease of devotional life.

As I sat in the church, meditating on the promise that we are to be a kingdom of *kohanim*, I started to dwell on the ministry of priests in the Old Testament. I reflected on the different parts of the Temple where they served, and how each part of that structure was associated symbolically with some aspect of worship and prayer. At some point or other during this time, I had what I can only describe as a 'eureka' moment. I suddenly sensed God saying to me, 'Why not use the layout of the Temple as a model of prayer? Why not try using the different stages of the journey into the Holy of Holies as stations of prayer?' The more I thought about that, the more excited I became. I realised that the Temple in Jerusalem had always been the place of meeting, encounter and presence. In the Old Testament era, God had used the Temple as the place of communion with himself. Now, in the New Testament era, the Temple in Jerusalem may no longer exist but the church is now called the

Temple of God's Holy Spirit and every believer is a part of God's royal priesthood. That being the case, the structure and service of the Jerusalem Temple can still have relevance for the believer's worship and prayer life today.

The Temple Ministries

At the heart of this book is the belief that the ministry of the Levitical priests in the Old Testament can serve as a useful model for Christian prayer in the twenty-first century. In 1 Chronicles 23:28 we read:

> The duty of the Levites was to help Aaron's descendants in the service of the temple of the Lord: to be in charge of the courtyards, the side rooms, the purification of all sacred things and the performance of other duties at the house of God.

I firmly believed 20 years ago, and I still believe it today, that the Holy Spirit wants to restore the ministry of the Levites to the Church. While this does not mean a literal re-enactment of their ministry, I do believe it could involve emulating their duties *metaphorically*.

In order to see just how this might be, we need to remind ourselves about the history and design of the Jerusalem Temple (or, more accurately, temples). There were in fact two temples in Jerusalem, one after the other. The first one was constructed by King Solomon in the middle of the tenth century BC (1 Kings 5—8; 2 Chronicles 3—4) and was destroyed by the Babylonians in 585 BC. The second Temple was built by those who returned from the Babylonian exile (Ezra 3:8–13) and was dedicated in 515 BC (Ezra 6:16–18). It was enlarged by Herod the Great in 20 BC and then completely destroyed by the Romans in AD 70.

The plan of the Temple followed the design of the Tabernacle, and looked like the diagram below.

The priest on duty would enter through the gates of thanksgiving. At the heart of the court of praise was the altar of sacrifice where he would offer sacrifices for the forgiveness of sins. Past that was the laver of water, a great bronze basin where the priest would wash before entering the holy place. This was illuminated by

THE TEMPLE

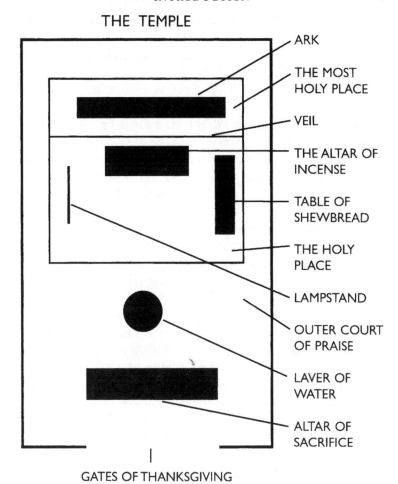

ARK

THE MOST
HOLY PLACE

VEIL

THE ALTAR OF
INCENSE

TABLE OF
SHEWBREAD

THE HOLY
PLACE

LAMPSTAND

OUTER COURT
OF PRAISE

LAVER OF
WATER

ALTAR OF
SACRIFICE

GATES OF THANKSGIVING

golden lampstands, known as the *menorah*, which had seven golden candlesticks. On the right-hand side of the Holy Place were the golden tables of shewbread where the priest presented and consecrated pieces of bread. At the heart of the Holy Place was the golden altar where the priest burnt incense in the morning and the evening. This incense represented the prayers of God's people ascending into heaven. Finally, beyond the veil, was the cherubim throne in the Most Holy Place. Only the high priest, once every year, was allowed to enter this innermost sanctuary.

What a great model or structure for personal prayer! Did Isaiah not prophesy a time when the Temple would be called '*a house of prayer* for all nations' (Isaiah 56:7)? Does Jesus himself not call the

Temple in Jerusalem 'a *house of prayer*' (Matthew 23:13)? Twenty years ago I was powerfully struck by how the God-given design of the Temple could be used as the basis for ministering to God in my own daily prayer life. I was struck by how God's Temple could be turned into what the prophet and the Messiah called 'a house of prayer'.

On that day back in the 1980s I tried a new way of praying. I began my prayer time by entering the gates of God's presence with thanksgiving. I then spent time in the court of praise, worshipping God for who he is. I then paused at the new altar of sacrifice, the Cross of Jesus, in order to confess my sins. I then washed at the laver of water before ascending the steps to the great entrance to the Holy Place. After this I spent time at the table of shewbread and the golden lampstands, petitioning for my daily physical and spiritual needs. I then proceeded to the golden altar of incense, to offer intercessions to God. Finally, I passed through the torn veil to enter the Most Holy Place, where it was believed one could see the throne of God. Here I spent time worshipping the Father.

That first day praying what I call the 'Temple model of prayer' was the beginning of a fresh intimacy with God. Today, I am still using this model in prayer. Though no two days are identical, the foundational pattern has remained the same, five stages of prayer corresponding to the five main ministry stations in the Temple:

1.   The Gates of Thanksgiving = Thanking God.
2.   The Court of Praise = Praising God.
3.   The Altar of Sacrifice = Repentance.
4.   The Altar of Incense = Intercession.
5.   The Most Holy Place = Beholding the Throne.

I have found time and time again that this basic design has held me in good stead, particularly at times when the pressures of life could have stifled my prayers altogether. While I appreciate that one person's prayer pattern can be another person's prison, this Temple model has never confined me. It has released me into a consistent practice of prayer in which I have drawn near to God – and he to me – many times. Two decades on, I still value this model as a gift from the Father.

The Benefits of this Model

As I have used this model, I have found a number of benefits in this approach to personal prayer. First of all, it is easy to remember. There is something about using the plan of a house, or any other kind of building, which appeals to the faculty of human memory. Somehow, using rooms and furniture as mnemonics is a very effective way of structuring what one wants to say. Thus ancient orators like Cicero, when they gave a speech in politics or in the law courts, used to remember everything they had prepared to say by using the model of a Roman house. The hall would be their introduction, and various items of decor in the hall would be used to represent various features of this introduction. So the process would go on: the speech would end once the speaker's mind had roamed through all the rooms in his imagined house of memory.

One of the reasons why people have found the Temple model helpful is because, like the Roman villa, it provides a basic structure for what one wants to say, and at the same time contains obvious mnemonics or memory aids. The gates of thanksgiving, for example, are where we pray prayers of thanksgiving; the altar of sacrifice is where we put sin to death, and so on. All the aspects of the Temple function as reminders of what we have to do as we minister to God in prayer.

Secondly, this way of praying appeals to the imagination. We all of us struggle to keep our imaginations under control when we pray. Hardly a moment passes before our minds are up to their old tricks again, putting images and fantasies of the most distracting nature before us. Perhaps this is why Simone Weil once wrote, in her book *Gravity and Grace*, that 'the imagination is constantly at work filling in the fissures through which grace would pass'.

However, focusing on a building as we go through stages of prayer is a very effective way of giving the imagination something else to think about! Many of the Christian mystics have discovered this to be true. I think in particular of Teresa of Avila who confessed to feeling 'exasperated' by the antics of her imagination in prayer. She described her imagination as 'restless, confused, and excited, and apparently not centred on God at all, in a word distracted'.[1] To combat this, Teresa came up with the idea of an 'interior castle' as a structure for daily prayer. Basing this model loosely on John 14, she built a castle of seven 'mansions'. These mansions represented different forms of prayer, the first beginning with preparatory disciplines, the last with prayer designed for the highest forms of union between us and the Father. So Teresa begins her classic work on prayer with the words,

> The soul seems to me to be like a castle,
> made of a single diamond or of very clear crystal
> in which there are many rooms,
> just as in heaven
> there are many mansions.[2]

Many others have found that using the image of a building or a house is of great benefit for undistracted prayer. Catherine of Sienna, for example, used to think of her soul as an inner cell of prayer. More recently, Andrew Murray used to speak of entering the inner chamber of the heart. These great men and women of prayer have used architectural symbolism in their prayer life as a means of directing the imagination away from the flesh. The Temple model of prayer is helpful for the same reasons.

A third benefit of the Temple model is that it is gradual. What do I mean by gradual? Today we live in an instant culture. We can tune into just about anything just by pressing a button. This has inevitably affected us as Christians. We do tend to tune into God straight away, to hurry into the Holy of Holies without any pause in our talk, any reverence in our step. There is a positive side to this in that it reveals confidence in our approach to the throne. It shows that we are certain of God's acceptance, sure of his welcome. However, there is a negative side too. It reveals a degree of over-familiarity and presumption. Instead of proceeding towards the innermost sanctuary with a holy fear, we rush in where angels fear to tread.

In the Temple in Jerusalem everything was designed to create a gradual and respectful approach to God. First of all, there was a division of the outer and inner areas of the Temple. In New Testament Greek this distinction is suggested by the two words which we translate as 'Temple'. The first is *hieron* which denotes the outer court or precincts of the Temple. The second is *naos*, which indicates the inner area – the sanctuary building where the Holy Place and the Holy of Holies were situated. Secondly, two different metals were used. In the outer court, most of the Temple furniture was fashioned out of bronze. The altar of sacrifice was made of bronze; the laver of water was also made of bronze. Once we enter the sanctuary building, the *naos*, everything changes. The candlesticks are made of gold. The table of shewbread is made of gold. The altar of incense is made of gold. Everywhere you look there is gold. The nearer you get to the Holy of Holies, the more precious, sacred and awesome is the experience.

The Temple model of prayer is therefore ideally suited for a gradual approach to God.

The Call to Priesthood

So the design of the Temple has proved invaluable in developing a priestly model of prayer. As St John saw, when he was caught up in the Spirit on the Island of Patmos, God has made us 'a kingdom *and* priests to serve our God' (Revelation 1:6). This is our destiny, this is our great vocation in the Lord Jesus Christ; to be both God's kingdom *and* God's priests. This calling is for all those who confess Jesus Christ as their Lord and Saviour. It is not just for an elite few. All can minister to the Father as priests of the Lord, female and male, old and young, Gentile and Jew. All can serve in the royal priesthood just as all can serve in God's Kingdom.

One reason why I have written this book is because in recent years we have heard a lot about the Kingdom, but we have not heard so much about the priesthood. We have heard a lot about preaching the Kingdom, healing the sick and delivering the demonised. We have heard less about ministering to God as priests in the holy Temple of his presence.

While I wholeheartedly support any emphasis on the Kingdom of God, I cannot endorse the neglect of the theme of priesthood. Too much emphasis on the Kingdom will bring an imbalance in favour of ministering *for* God. Yet we are also called to minister *to* him. While we all should desire to do the works of the Kingdom – preaching, evangelising, healing, setting the captives free, and so forth – we cannot do this effectively if we are not prioritising our ministry of worship and prayer. Too much emphasis on the Kingdom will result in an excess in doing. But we are also called simply to be. We are invited to remember that Martha's choice was a good one (serving Jesus) but Mary's was the best (sitting at Jesus' feet in adoration).

My prayer is that by the end of our journey through this book, we will have made a decision to live out our priesthood, and to say with King David,

> One thing I ask of the LORD,
> this is what I seek:
> that I may dwell in the house of the LORD
> all the days of my life,
> to gaze upon the beauty of the LORD
> and to seek him in his temple.
>
> Psalm 27:4

Prayer

Heavenly Father, I thank you that you have called me to the royal priesthood. I thank you that my greatest priority is to minister to you in the Temple of your holy presence. As I come to prayer now, I ask you to increase the anointing for priesthood upon my life. I ask you to help me through the stages of prayer – the gates of thanksgiving, the courts of praise, the altar of incense, the Holy Place, the innermost sanctuary. Lead me by your Spirit into the very heart of your holy presence. Help me to draw near to you in intimate communion. I pray this in the name of Jesus, our Great High Priest. Amen.

ONE

Preparing for the Journey

The first rule of true prayer is to have heart and mind in the right mood for talking with God.
John Calvin, *Institutes*

Before we look at the first stage of the Temple model of prayer – the gates of thanksgiving – it is good to emphasise right at the outset the vital role of the Holy Spirit in this method of praying. The Temple model of prayer is a great structure but as with all structures, there is always a danger that the form may quench the fire. It is one thing having a tidy fireplace. It is another thing altogether having a fire burning in the grate. The Temple model of prayer will only prove to be a great asset if the Holy Spirit is allowed to move within this structure. We must always seek to invite the Holy Spirit to lead us in our prayers and to give us that divine freedom within this orderly framework.

In a sense, this is how God has always chosen to work. Yes, the Father loves design, order, symmetry and structure. In Exodus 25—27 God instructed Moses about the furniture and the framework for the Tabernacle – the prototype for the Temple. At the same time, this structure was to be the place in which his Spirit dwelt. In Exodus 25:8 God says, 'I want the people of Israel to build me a sacred residence where I can live among them.' The *mikdash* (sanctuary) of the *mishkan* (Tabernacle) was always designed to be the place for God's *shakan* (habitation). Thus, at the end of the Book of Exodus, we see the glory cloud of God's presence filling the Tabernacle:

> Then the cloud covered the Tabernacle, and the glorious presence of the LORD filled it. Moses was no longer able to enter the Tabernacle because the cloud had settled down over it, and the Tabernacle was filled with the awesome glory of the LORD.
>
> Exodus 40:34–35

What was true for the Tabernacle was also true for the Temple, whose basic design was the same as the Tabernacle. Here again, the structure was supposed to be the place of God's Spirit. The house was supposed to be the locus of God's presence. So, after King

Solomon has built the first Temple, he prays that God may come and dwell in the Temple sanctuary:

> O my God, be attentive to all the prayers made to you in this place. And now, O LORD God, arise and enter this resting place of yours, where your magnificent Ark has been placed. May your priests, O LORD God, be clothed with salvation, and may your saints rejoice in your goodness.
>
> 2 Chronicles 6:40–41

In answer to Solomon's prayer, fire came down from heaven and the glory cloud of God's presence filled the Temple, overwhelming the priests on duty there.

Today, of course, there is no Temple in Jerusalem. The Church has replaced the physical structure of the Temple and is now the place in which God's Holy Spirit is to be found. Individually, our bodies – as believers – are likened to temples filled with God's Spirit. Corporately, believers form a people likened to God's house. As Paul wrote in Ephesians 2:20–22:

> We are his house, built on the foundation of the apostles and the prophets. And the cornerstone is Christ Jesus himself. We who believe are carefully joined together, becoming a holy temple for the Lord. Through him you Gentiles are also joined together as part of this dwelling where God lives by his Spirit.

All of this serves to highlight the great importance of making sure that our spirits are attuned to God's Holy Spirit as we begin our prayer time. Before anything else, we should welcome the Holy Spirit. As Raniero Cantalamessa has rightly said:

> The very best way to start a prayer time is by asking the Holy Spirit to unite us with the prayer of Jesus. Jesus as we see him in the Gospels used to pray at all times of the day: early in the morning, in the evening, at night. When we turn to prayer at one or other of these times, we can simply put ourselves at Jesus' side as he prays and let the Spirit carry on praising and blessing the Father in us. There is a hidden power in all of this

that we come to know only when we consistently put it into practice.[1]

There's a Battle On

Why is it so important to invite the Holy Spirit to come and fill the fireplace with his holy fire? One answer is because a fierce spiritual battle takes place every time we choose to spend time alone with the Father in prayer. On at least three fronts we are pulled away from entering into that secret place of intimacy with the Father, and we need power beyond our natural strength to resist these soul-destroying forces. That power is available to every believer. Paul, in his own prayer life, prayed for Christians in his churches that they would experience the incomparable greatness of God's power (Ephesians 1:17). He prayed this because he knew there was a spiritual battle and that all Christians need to be strong with the Lord's mighty power (Ephesians 6:10). We need this power today, and the good news is that it is available to those who ask (Luke 11:13).

What then are these forces we have to contend against in prayer? They are three – the world, the flesh and the devil.

The world pulls us away from prayer because it constantly sets before us a whole variety of distractions. Some of these are the distractions of noise. John Donne knew this only too well. He once said, 'I throw myself down in my room, and I invite God and His angels thither; and when they come there, I neglect God for the noise of a fly, the rattle of a coach and the whining of a door.'[2] Other distractions come in the form of tasks which clamour for our attention. The world says, 'You haven't got time to pray today. There's too much to do in the home, at the office, wherever.'

The flesh pulls us away from prayer because, as Richard Lovelace puts it, 'our fallen nature is actually allergic to God'.[3] The constant inclination of our flesh is towards self-sufficiency. Our spirits, when joined to God's Holy Spirit, incline in the opposite direction. They tell us that self-sufficiency is sin, that we are called to be dependent upon an all-sufficient God. The basic instinct of the flesh is therefore hostile to prayer. The flesh needs to be subdued if we are to meet with the Father.

If the world and the flesh pull us away from prayer, so does the devil. The devil in fact hates us praying because he knows the awesome power that is released against him even in our feeblest prayers. As Matilda Andross once said,

> prayer is more powerful than habits, heredity, and natural tendencies. It can overcome all these. It is more powerful than the forces that hold the planets in place. Prayer, though it comes from the heart of an unlearned child of God, can suspend the laws of the universe, if such be God's will, just as the sun stood still when Joshua prayed. There is no other power on earth that the enemy of souls hates and fears as he does prayer. We are told that 'Satan trembles when he sees the weakest saint upon his knees.' No wonder the enemy of our souls fights so hard to prevent us from praying. Jim Cymbala puts it well: 'the devil is not terribly frightened of our human efforts and credentials. But he knows his kingdom will be damaged when we begin to lift up our hearts to God.'

With the world, the flesh and the devil obstructing our path to prayer, the odds are stacked against us right from the start. This shows how important it is to ask God's Holy Spirit to combat the work of these three enemies of prayer. We need to invite the Holy Spirit to come and empower us for prayer. As Andrew Murray encourages us:

> The great lesson for every prayer is – see to it, first of all, that you commit yourself to the leading of the Holy Spirit, and with entire dependence on Him, give Him the first place; for through Him your prayer will have a value you cannot imagine, and through Him also you will learn to speak out your desires in the name of Christ.[4]

The best place to begin with the Temple model of prayer is accordingly the invocation of the Holy Spirit. To quote one of the ancient hymns of the Church (*Veni Creator Spiritus*):

> Come, Creator Spirit
> Visit the minds of those who are yours;
> Fill with heavenly grace
> The hearts that you have made.

The God of Surprises

We begin our prayers with what the theologians call the *epiklesis* (invocation of the Holy Spirit) in order to override the destructive inclinations of the world, the flesh and the devil. We also invoke the Holy Spirit so that we can enjoy supernatural spontaneity in our prayers. This is important because the Temple model of prayer is overtly structural in character. We begin with the gates of thanksgiving, we then enter the court of praise, we pause at the altar of sacrifice, wash at the laver of water, enter the Holy Place, make petitions at the table of shewbread and the golden lampstands, intercede at the altar of incense, before entering the Holy of Holies in an attitude of devotional prayer. All this involves a framework, a plan, a structure.

Structure is, of course, helpful, especially when one is exhausted and weak. As T. S. Eliot said of poetry, 'Organization is necessary as well as inspiration.'[5] What is true of poetry is also true of prayer. In prayer we do need some kind of mental super-structure to provide the outline and direction for what we do. However, the reverse of what T. S. Eliot said is also true: 'Inspi-ration is necessary as well as organization.' Relying too much on structure is an obstacle to what the rabbis called *hitla-havaut* – fervour in prayer.[6] Structure can actually quench the Spirit from revealing the mind of Christ to us. That is why we must begin by asking the Holy Spirit to bring revelation and power to our prayers. Without the touch of God's Spirit, we will never encounter the God of surprises.

There is a story in Scripture which illustrates this well. The first chapter of Luke's Gospel records some experiences of John the Baptist's father, Zechariah. According to Luke, Zechariah was a priest. He was a very godly man who observed all the Lord's commandments and regulations. One day, Zechariah was chosen to be the one who went into the Temple sanctuary to burn incense at the golden altar in the holy place. Zechariah with due reverence went in to perform his priestly duty, while everyone else waited outside in the court of praise, worshipping God.

All, at first, went smoothly. Zechariah went to the table of shewbread and placed new loaves upon it. He went to the golden candlesticks, put new candles in and lit them. He then went to the golden altar, placed new incense on the censers and lit that. As the smoke ascended to the roof of the Temple, Zechariah started his priestly liturgy, his hands raised towards heaven. At that moment, Luke says – in a somewhat matter-of-fact way, as if it were a common occurrence – 'an angel appeared to Zechariah'. This angel materialised at the right-hand side of the altar where Zechariah was praying. Zechariah, says Luke, was 'startled', which, of course, is an understatement. However, the angel reassured Zechariah, and told him some good and unexpected news about becoming a father – a message which no doubt startled Zechariah because of his old age.

Zechariah showed a distinct lack of faith at this point – not surprisingly, since in his eyes he had passed the age of fathering children – and he subsequently earned a rebuke from the angel, who revealed that he was Gabriel. The rebuke involved a punishment: Zechariah would not be able to speak again until the child was born. And so Zechariah came out of the Temple to find the crowds waiting, wondering why it was that he had spent so long doing what was a routine, liturgical duty. They would be none the wiser for a while, because Zechariah's lips had been supernaturally sealed. So Zechariah returned home to his wife Elizabeth and found his voice again only when his baby, John the Baptist, was born.

This episode cautions us against regarding our daily ministry to God as a routine task. Ministering to God in the Temple of prayer is the very opposite of that. We too may be surprised by God. We too may experience a strong anointing or burden from the Holy Spirit. We too may receive a prophetic word for the Church. We may even come face to face with an angel.

And so the opening *epiklesis*, the opening invocation of the Holy Spirit, is a vital ingredient in our prayer time. It makes room for God to move in whatever way he sovereignly chooses. It makes room for the God of surprises.

Surprised by Joy

Many Christians during the course of history have been surprised by joy in the midst of their private prayers. Richard Rolle, the medieval Christian mystic, had an extraordinary experience of God's Holy Spirit in the church in Hampole. Though the date of his experiences is obscure (some time in the early 1300s), the nature of it is not. This is what Rolle experienced:

> I cannot tell you how surprised I was the first time I felt my heart begin to warm. It was real warmth too, not imaginary, and it felt as if it were actually on fire. I was astonished at the way the heat surged up, and how this new sensation brought great and unexpected comfort.
>
> I was sitting in a certain chapel, delighting in the sweetness of prayer or meditation, when suddenly I felt within myself an unusually pleasant heat. At first I wondered where it came from, but it was not long before I realized that it was from none of his creatures but from the Creator himself . . . While I was sitting in that same chapel, and repeating as best I could the night-psalms before I went in to supper, I heard above my head it seemed, the joyful ring of psalmody, or perhaps I should say, the singing. In my prayer I was reaching out to heaven with heartfelt longing when I became aware, in a way I cannot explain, of a symphony of song, and in myself I sensed a corresponding harmony at once wholly delectable and heavenly, which persisted in my mind . . . The effect of this inner sweetness was that I began to sing what previously I had spoken: only I sang inwardly, and that for my Creator.[7]

Rolle experienced the fire of God's love in the ordinariness of his daily devotions. He experienced a warmth from heaven (*calor* in Latin) that resulted in songs of praise in his heart (*canor*). Put differently, the Holy Spirit surprised and delighted Richard Rolle in the normality of his daily spiritual disciplines. Like Zechariah in the Temple, Rolle was visited by God in God's house.

But it is not just those who pray in church buildings that experience the fire of God's love. Hans Nielsen Hauge, Norway's equivalent of John Wesley, experienced a tremendous wave of God's love while worshipping as he ploughed his father's field. Later on he wrote of this 1796 experience as if it had been yesterday:

> One time, as I was working in the open air, I was singing off by heart the hymn 'Jesus, to taste your sweet abiding presence, etc.' When I had sung the second verse:

> Strengthen me really powerfully in my soul,
> So I can discover what the Spirit is capable of,
> Take me captive in my speech and my mind,
> Lead me and draw me as weak as I am;
> My self and what is mine I will gladly lose,
> If you alone will live in my soul,
> And at last whatever disturbs my heartfelt peace
> Must slip away through the door.

> Then my mind was so uplifted to God, that I could not sense, nor can express what took place in my soul; for I was out of myself, and it was only when my thoughts gathered themselves, that I was sorry I hadn't served the beloved, good God, who is over all things, and I now thought nothing in the world was of any regard. That my soul felt something supernatural, divine and blessed; that there was a glory that no tongue can express, is something I remember so clearly to this day, as if it had happened a few days ago, although however 20 years have now passed since God's love visited me so abundantly.[8]

This experience of the Holy Spirit propelled Hauge into a nation-wide revival ministry in Norway, resulting in thousands coming to know Jesus Christ.

If Rolle was surprised by God in a church, and Hauge in a field, Charles Finney, the great nineteenth-century American revivalist, was filled with the Holy Spirit while behind closed doors in his office at work. In 1821 he experienced the following:

> As I went in and shut the door after me, it seemed as if I met the Lord Jesus Christ face to face . . . it seemed to me a reality, He stood before me, and I fell down at His feet and poured out my soul to Him . . . the Holy Spirit descended upon me in a manner that seemed to go through me, body and soul. I could feel the impression, like a wave of electricity, going through and through me. Indeed, it seemed to come in waves and waves of liquid love; for I could not express it in any other way. These waves came over me, and over me, and over me, one after the other, until I recollect I cried out, 'I shall die if these waves continue to pass over me.' I said, 'Lord I cannot bear any more'; yet I had no fear of death . . .[9]

Finally, coming nearer to our present time, one of the world's leading Pentecostal theologians, Professor J. Rodman Williams (author of the three-volume *Renewal Theology*) describes his own experience at his desk, as he was preparing a lecture on the doctrine of God in 1965:

Then came Wednesday, the day before Thanksgiving – THE DAY! I felt at ease, and began to turn to letters on my desk. One letter was from a pastor who described his experience of recently visiting the seminary and being prayed for by a student to receive the gift of the Holy Spirit. He wrote about how later he began to speak in tongues and praise God mightily. As I read and re-read the letter, the words somehow seemed to leap off the page, and I found myself being overcome. I was soon on my knees practically in tears praying for the Holy Spirit, and pounding on the chair – asking, seeking, knocking – in a way I never had done before. *Now I intensely yearned for the gift of the Holy Spirit.* Then I stood and began to beseech God to break me open, to fill me to the fullest – with sometimes an almost torturous cry to what was in myself to possess my total being. But for a time all seemed to no avail. With hands outstretched I then began to pray to God the Father, Son, and Holy Spirit – and mixed in with the entreaty was a verse of Scripture I kept crying out: 'Bless the Lord, O my soul; and all that is within me, bless his holy name!'

I yearned to bless the Lord with *all* my being – my total self, body, soul, and spirit – *all* that was within me. Then I knew it was happening: *I was being filled with His Holy Spirit.* Also, for the first time I earnestly desired to speak in tongues because the English language seemed totally incapable of expressing the inexpressible glory and love of God. Instead of articulating rational words I began to ejaculate sounds of any kind, praying that somehow the Lord would use them. Suddenly I realized that something drastic was happening: my noises were being left behind, and I was off with such utterance, such words as I had never heard before.

Wave after wave, torrent after torrent, poured out. It was utterly fantastic. I was doing it and yet I was not. I seemed to be utterly detached and utterly involved. To some degree I could control the speed of the words – but not much; they

were pouring out at a terrific rate. I could stop the flow whenever I wanted, but in operation I had absolutely no control
over the nature or articulation of the sounds. My tongue, my
jaws, my vocal chords were totally possessed – but not by me.
Tears began to stream down my face – joy unutterable,
amazement incredible. Over and over I felt borne down to the
floor by the sheer weight of it all – and sometimes I would
cry: 'I don't believe it; I don't believe it!' It was so completely unlike anything I had ever known before.

Finally, I sat down in my chair, but still felt buoyed up as if
by a vast inner power. I knew I was on earth, but it was as if
heaven had intersected it – and I was in both. God was so
much there that I scarcely moved a muscle: His delicate, lush,
ineffable presence.[10]

Praying in a church, praying in a field, praying in an office at work,
praying at a desk at home – here are just some of the many contexts
in which ordinary people have been visited by God in extraordinary ways. Though the experiences may not be identical, they
all exhibit one common truth: that the Holy Spirit can move with
great freedom in the common framework of our private prayers.

Our Priority in Prayer

So the first task in prayer is to welcome the person and the power
of the Holy Spirit. As you sit, walk, kneel or stand, invite the Holy
Spirit to come and light the fire again in your heart. Ask him to
come and seize your heart with the power of a great affection. Ask
the Father to make your body once again a temple full of the Holy
Spirit, and pray for the leading of the Holy Spirit at all stages in
your journey into the Most Holy Place.

Whether you are sat at home at your desk, in the kitchen, at the
office, on a walk, or in a church building, the Father is longing to
draw near to those who draw near to him. Ask him to empower you
to fulfil your vocation as a priest in the Kingdom of God. Pray for
the Father to enable you to minister to him in a way that thrills his
heart.

In addition, pray for protection against every ungodly distrac-
tion and interruption. Put on the whole armour of God and be
strong in the Lord and the power of his might. Remember there is

a battle on and resolve to resist the pull of the flesh, the world and the devil.

Finally, pray in the Spirit. If you have the gift of tongues, start praying in the Spirit as you welcome the presence of the Lord. The gift of tongues is a great resource in personal prayer. As we speak to the Father in the language of the angels, our minds and hearts are tuned into the frequency of heaven.

Prayer

Father, I thank you so much for this opportunity to meet with you. I invite you now to come and fill my heart with the fire of your love. Come, Holy Spirit, in Jesus' name. I welcome your presence. Anoint me as a priest once again. Help me to minister to the Father in spirit and in truth. Lead me, to the very heart of the Father in the Most Holy Place. Make my body right now a temple of the Holy Spirit.

I thank you, Father, that you call us to stand in the spiritual battle. Thank you that you urge us to be more than conquerors and enable us to overcome. I put on the full armour of God right now – the belt of truth, the shoes of the Gospel of peace, the breastplate of righteousness, the helmet of salvation, the shield of faith and the sword of the Spirit, the Word of God. I resolve to stand firm in you, Lord, and in the power of your might.

Come down, O love divine.

Give me a time of uninterrupted space and grace in which to meet the Father.

Keep all ungodly distractions and interruptions from me.

Help me to enter in to the fullness of what you desire for me right now.

In the name of Jesus, our Great High Priest, Amen.

The Gates of Thanksgiving

Even if our mouths were filled with songs like the sea, our tongues with joy like its mighty waves, our lips with praise like the breadth of the sky, if our eyes shone like the sun and the moon, and our hands were spread out like the eagles of heaven, if our feet were as swift as the hind, we should still be incapable of thanking you adequately for one thousandth part of all the love You have shown us.
A Jewish Passover prayer

Once we have made the person of the Holy Spirit welcome, we are ready to enter the gates of thanksgiving, one of three thresholds we will cross as we proceed through the Temple model of prayer, drawing near to the Father. The first threshold is the entrance to the court of praise; the second is the entrance to the Holy Place; the third is the entrance to the Holy of Holies.

As we pause at the gates of thanksgiving, it is helpful to remember the exhortation in Psalm 100:4: 'Enter his gates with thanksgiving and his courts with praise; give thanks to him and praise his name.' Here the psalmist is using the design of the Temple as a model for approaching God in worship. He knows that the first two stages of the journey into the sanctuary are the entrance to the inner court of the priests, which he describes as 'the gates of thanksgiving', and the courts themselves, which he calls 'the courts of praise'.

While this is probably an example of Hebrew parallelism – saying the same thing in two slightly different ways – many people find it helpful to distinguish between thanksgiving and praise. Although it may be a slightly artificial division (in terms of the psalmist's understanding), thanksgiving has to do with God's acts; praise has to do with God's being. In thanksgiving, we thank God for what he has done. In praise, we worship God for who he is.

In thanking God we therefore focus on God's deeds – the revelation of his Name, the Exodus, the giving of the Law, the promise of the Messiah, the Incarnation, the Cross, the Resurrection, the giving of the Spirit. In praising God we focus on God's character and nature – his beauty, his majesty, his mercy, his holiness, his power, his otherness, his love, his compassion, his bounty, his faithfulness, his greatness and his truth.

In many places the Bible stresses the importance of thanksgiving. The Old Testament is full of heartfelt expressions of gratitude to God. The Book of Psalms is a particularly rich reservoir of gratitude:

Psalm 7:17: 'I will give thanks to the Lord because of his righteousness . . .'

Psalm 28:7: 'My heart leaps for joy and I will give thanks to him in song . . .'

Psalm 35:18: 'I will give you thanks in the great assembly . . .'

Psalm 75:1: 'We give thanks to you, O God, we give thanks for your Name is near . . .'

Psalm 107:1: 'Give thanks to the Lord for he is good . . .'

Psalm 118:28: 'You are my God, and I will give you thanks . . .'

Clearly, thanksgiving was an essential part of prayer for King David (who wrote many of the psalms). Gratitude is the true response to God's enduring goodness.

What is true for David is true for his son Solomon. Solomon, like David, often burst enthusiastically into thanksgiving known as a *berakah*, a prayer which begins with the words 'Blessed be God': 'Blessed be the Lord, the God of Israel, who with his own hand has fulfilled what he promised with his own mouth to my father David' (1 Kings 8:15). The same dedication ends with a *berakah* of thankfulness: 'Blessed be the Lord, who has given rest to his people Israel just as he promised' (1 Kings 8:56).

This use of the *berakah*, it should be noted, is found in the psalms as well. Indeed, each of the books of the Psalter concludes with a *berakah* to the Lord (Psalms 41:13; 72:8, 19; 89:52; 106:48).

This Old Testament emphasis on gratitude left its mark on Jewish prayer. The most important formula of prayer in the Jewish liturgy became the *berakah*. This word literally means 'blessing' and is always a prayer of thanks. Here are a few examples: before drinking a glass of wine, a Jew will say, 'Blessed art thou, O Lord our God, King of the Universe, who createst the fruit of the vine.' Before eating bread, a Jew will exclaim, 'Blessed art thou, O Lord our God, King of the Universe, who bringest forth bread from the earth.'

Before reading the Torah, a Jew will pray, 'Blessed art thou, O Lord our God, King of the Universe, who hast given us the Law of truth, and hast planted everlasting life in our midst. Blessed art thou, O Lord, Giver of the Torah.'

Blessing God for his gifts is therefore a characteristic of Jewish prayer. Indeed, one of the 18 benedictions recited regularly in the

Jewish synagogues is a fine example of this desire to thank the
Lord for his gracious blessings:

> We give thanks unto thee, for thou art the Lord our God and
> the God of our fathers for ever and ever; thou art the Rock of
> our lives, the Shield of our salvation through every genera-
> tion. We will give thanks unto thee and declare thy praise for
> our lives which are committed unto thy hand and for our
> souls which are in thy charge, and for thy miracles which are
> daily with us, and for thy wonders and thy benefits, which are
> wrought at all times, evening, morn and noon. O thou who art
> all good, whose mercies fail not; thou merciful Being, whose
> loving kindnesses never cease, we have ever hoped in thee.
> Blessed art thou, O Lord, whose Name is all-good, and unto
> whom it is becoming to give thanks.[1]

The Need to be Grateful

As we turn to the Gospels, we find gratitude everywhere. This
should not surprise us; Jesus himself was a Jew, and he would have
heard many a *berakah* during his life. He would also have known
those many commands to thank God, whose presence we have
noted in the Hebrew Bible.

Jesus' prayers to his Father are sometimes expressed in the form
of a *berakah*. One famous example is in Matthew 11:25 (Luke
10:21), when Jesus thanks God for the spiritual insights which
Peter has just shown:

> I thank thee, Father, Lord of heaven and earth, that thou hast
> hidden these things from the wise and understanding and
> revealed them to babes.

In all probability, this prayer originally began with the formula,
'Blessed art thou'.

Likewise, when Jesus gave thanks for the bread with which he
fed the five thousand, he almost certainly would have used a
berakah (Mark 6:41). Other examples can be found in the narra-
tives concerning the institution of the Eucharist (Mark 14:22–4
and parallels). At the Last Supper, Jesus would have recited a
berakah after he had taken the bread (or the wine). In our versions

we simply read 'he blessed it' but in reality this would have been a prayer of thanksgiving, beginning 'Blessed art thou, O Lord our God . . .'

If Jesus practised thanksgiving, he also preached it. We know this from a short story told only in Luke's Gospel (17:11–19). Here we see Jesus travelling on the border between Samaria and Galilee. He is about to enter a village when ten men with leprosy shout out, 'Jesus, Master, have pity on us!' They are on the outskirts of the village because lepers were not allowed any nearer to habitation than that. Jesus does indeed have pity on them. He tells them to go and show themselves to the priests. If someone was a leper, he only showed himself to a priest if he had been healed of leprosy. So the fact that the ten immediately go and do so shows not only that they are obedient (because they go), it shows that they are full of faith (because they believe without any tangible evidence).

As they leave for their local priests, the story rather tersely remarks that 'they were cleansed'. That means that they were healed as they walked. Nine of them carry on their journey. One decides to come running back to Jesus. He throws himself at Jesus' feet and thanks him. That man, says Luke, was not a Jew; he was a Samaritan.

At this point, Jesus speaks out. He says, 'Where are the other nine of you? There were ten healed. Are you the only to come back and say thank you? Where are the thankless nine?'

Clearly, Jesus not only practised thanksgiving, he also preached it. His words in Luke's story show how vital it is for Christians not only to be a people of obedience (who 'go' when Jesus says 'go') and a people of faith (who 'believe' without seeing) but also a people of gratitude (who come back to Jesus to say 'thank you'). Where were the nine lepers who failed to say thank you? Why did they fail to return and express their gratitude? Charles Brown has speculated the reasons why:

> One waited to see if the cure was real.
> One waited to see if it would last.
> One said he would see Jesus later.
> One decided that he had never had leprosy.
> One said he would have gotten well anyway.
> One gave the glory to the priests.
> One said, 'O, well, Jesus didn't really do anything.'

One said, 'Any rabbi could have done it.'
One said, 'I was already much improved.'[2]

Maybe we can hear something of our selves in one or two of these excuses!

The Gratitude Attitude

But thanksgiving is not confined to Jesus alone in the New Testament. When we move on from the Gospels, we find that thanksgiving figures prominently in the writings of Paul. The New Testament word for *berakah* is *eucharistia*, from which we get 'Eucharist'. *Eucharistia* means thanksgiving, a word found often in the letters of Paul. For example, Paul uses the Greek verb *eucharisteo* when he speaks of the necessity of gratitude in the lifestyle of the Christian disciple. Christians are to have a 'gratitude attitude'. As Paul puts it in Colossians 3:17: 'Whatever you do, whether in word or deed, do it all in the name of the Lord Jesus, *giving thanks* (*eucharisteo*) to God the Father through him.' Earlier in this letter, Paul urges his readers to be 'overflowing with thankfulness' (*eucharistia*, Colossians 2:7), to revel in the use of *berakah*.

Paul stresses that this grateful heart is particularly important in the discipline of prayer. He exhorts the Colossian church members to 'devote yourselves to prayer, being watchful *and thankful*' (*eucharistia*, 4:2). In Philippians 4:6, he says, 'Do not be anxious about anything, but in everything, by prayer and petition, with thanksgiving (*eucharistia*), present your requests to God.'

Thanksgiving is therefore vital to prayer. According to the overall teaching of the New Testament, we are all priests, and we are all called to exercise a eucharistic ministry, to begin our prayers with the ministry of thanksgiving. As Andrew Murray puts it: 'Thanksgiving will draw our hearts out to God and keep us engaged with Him; it will take our attention from ourselves and give the Spirit room in our hearts.'[3] Thanksgiving, one might say, is the 'open sesame' into God's holy presence.

How then do we grow in the art of thanksgiving? If we look again at the word *eucharistia*, or thanksgiving, we shall discover an answer. Tucked away in the centre of *eucharistia* is the beautiful word *charis*, which means grace. Grace, one might say, is at the heart of gratitude. *Charis* is at the centre of *eucharistia*. This highlights the fact that our level of gratitude will exist in proportion to our awareness of God's grace. The more we are conscious of God's grace, the more grateful we will be. The less conscious we are of his grace, the less it will be natural for us to thank him with joy.

It is helpful, then, to meditate on God's unmerited love for us before we start trying to thank him. Once we remember that God has loved us to death on the Cross, and that this love is totally free and undeserved, we will find it easier to be grateful. Once we catch sight of the amazing grace of God, crying out from the tortured face of Jesus, we can never be ungrateful.

To be a truly grateful people we therefore need to focus on grace. It is sinful to be ungrateful in the presence of such a gracious Father. As King Lear exclaims, 'How sharper than a serpent's tooth it is to have a thankless child'. If we are not to wound our Heavenly Father with the sharp sting of ingratitude, we must constantly remind ourselves of his grace.

How Can I Give Thanks to God?

Perhaps at this point I can begin to share what I have learned over the years using the Temple model of prayer.

Every day, as I pass through the gates of thanksgiving, I find it helpful to base my prayers of gratitude on the words of John 1:16: 'Out of the fullness of God's grace, we have all received one blessing after another.'

This is a magnificent reminder of the extravagant grace of God. God is not miserly. He does not hold to a single- or a second-blessing theology. Our God believes in giving us continual blessings, 'one blessing after another'.

What, then, are those many blessings for which we can give thanks to God? Here it is important to develop a holistic view of grace. In other words, it is important to develop a worldview in which we are able to discern traces of God's grace in every part of our lives, not just in the spiritual things. We need to learn to give thanks for the blessings we have received in the physical, the emotional, the intellectual, the material, the relational as well as the spiritual dimensions of life. Nothing is too small, too insignificant, too profane, too worldly. The Father loves to be thanked for everything!

In this matter we have much to learn from the Jewish people. Unlike modern, Gentile Christians, the Jewish people have never restricted God's blessings to the spiritual sphere of life. In the Hebraic mindset there is simply no division between the sacred and the mundane. They have set prayers of thanksgiving for almost everything because they see the whole universe as a sanctuary of God's benediction. There is no place, no time, no activity, which is immune from thanksgiving. From a Jewish perspective, one can give thanks to God for anything, anytime, anyhow, anywhere.

Jewish liturgy is full of examples of this holistic understanding of gratitude. Berakhot 54a, in the Mishnah, reminds the Jewish people that:

> One who sees a place where miracles have been worked on behalf of Israel should say: 'Blessed is he who worked miracles for our fathers in this place.'

> One who sees a place in which a foreign worship was rooted out should say: 'Blessed is he who rooted foreign worship out of our land.'

> Of comets, storms, thunder, wind and lightning, one should say: 'Blessed is he whose strength and power fill the world.'

> Of mountains, hills, rivers and deserts one should say: 'Blessed is he who accomplishes the work of creation.'[4]

Our first ministry after welcoming the Holy Spirit is thanksgiving. In this ministry we look at every aspect of our lives since we last prayed and offer up thanks. 1 Timothy 4:3 says, 'Everything God created is good, and nothing is to be rejected if it is received with thanksgiving (*eucharistia*), because it is consecrated by the word of God and prayer.' The first duty of prayer is to give thanks to the Father for every evidence of his goodness in our lives. We literally count all our blessings. We exclude nothing. We bless the God who blesses us.

There are, generally speaking, six kinds of blessing which – in my experience – encourage and evoke our thanksgiving.

Spiritual Blessings

It is important not to neglect our spiritual blessings. In particular, it is essential to remember to thank the Father that we have a relationship with him at all. It should never cease to excite us that we can pray with the Lord of heaven and earth because he pursued us into a personal relationship with him. It should be a constant source of gratitude that God has, because of his grace, established a relationship of intimacy with us. This is the best of all God's blessings.

The poet, Coleridge, expressed this thought very powerfully a few days before he died:

> I have known what the enjoyments and advantages of this life are, and what the more refined pleasures which learning and intellectual power can bestow; and with all the experience that more than threescore years can give, I now, on the eve of my departure, declare to you . . . that health is a great blessing, competence obtained by honourable industry a great blessing, and a great blessing it is to have kind, faithful, and loving friends and relatives; but that the greatest of all blessings, as it is the most enabling of all privileges, is to be indeed a Christian.[5]

One of the finest prayers of thanksgiving for spiritual blessings can be found in Ephesians 1:3–14. These 12 verses form a single sentence in Greek; indeed, it is 26 lines long in the United Bible Societies' text. Clearly, Paul was so effusive in his gratitude to God that he lost his usual control of grammar. Ephesians 1:3–14 is a torrent of thanksgiving! Paul begins his *berakah* with the words:

> Blessed be the God and Father of our Lord Jesus Christ, who has blessed us in the heavenly realms with every spiritual blessing in Christ.

Here the thanksgiving is focused on the blessings received from God the Father. In the next nine verses, the thanksgiving is focused on the blessings received through God the Son (vv. 4–13a). Paul literally overflows with his grounds for gratitude:

he chose us in him before the creation of the world . . .
in love he predestined us . . .
in him we have redemption . . .
he made known to us the mystery of his pleasure . . .
in him we were also chosen . . .
and you were also included!

In the third part of the *berakah*, Paul's thanksgiving is focused upon the blessings received through God the Spirit (vv. 13b–14): 'you were marked in him with a seal, the promised Holy Spirit . . .'

Paul's prayer is a fine example of how to count one's spiritual blessings. It is thoroughly trinitarian; it rejoices in the blessings from the Father, blessings from the Son, blessings from the Holy Spirit. It is magnificently broad in sweep, going right back to the beginning of creation, and extending forward to the very end of the world, when the times will have reached their fulfilment (v. 10). There can surely be few finer examples of thanksgiving in the whole of Christian literature.

At the centre of Paul's prayer of gratitude is grace. At the midpoint of the passage, Paul speaks about the 'riches of God's grace that he *lavished* on us with all wisdom and understanding'. Paul is particularly grateful for God's grace because 'In love he predestined us to be adopted as his sons through Christ Jesus' (v. 5). For Paul, the reality of adoption forms the centre of his gratitude.

If that was true for Paul, it has also been true for me. Nothing puts me in touch with the true depths of God's grace more quickly than remembering that I am an adopted child of God. I relate to this metaphor of adoption because I am, in human terms, an adopted child. My twin sister and I were orphaned at birth and adopted by my present parents, Philip and Joy. Claire and I know nothing at all of our natural family. The bonding with Philip and Joy has not been painless but it is strong. I have written about this extensively in my book, *From Orphans to Heirs: Celebrating your Spiritual Adoption*.[6]

At the very centre of my soul there is a very strong appreciation of the fact that I was an orphan, that I could have remained an orphan, and that my life could have gone in many far less privileged directions. This has profoundly influenced my ability to thank God for his grace. Paul speaks in Ephesians 1:5 of a Father who predestined us to be adopted as his sons and daughters.

Through the love and the grace of God, we are made the brothers and sisters of Jesus and the children of God. We are given a new, Christ-centred family.

If you have been happily adopted yourself, this kind of theology strikes some very deep chords. You suddenly begin to see things very clearly: God is the perfect Father who looked out across the world he had made and saw his children as spiritual orphans. He saw them wandering aimlessly in sin, suffering from what Peter Berger calls 'a sense of homelessness in the cosmos'. What was he to do?

What he did was this: he asked his Son Jesus to come into the orphanage of our world in order to adopt us into his family. When Jesus said to his disciples, 'I will not leave you orphans' (John 14:18), he was expressing the very heart of God. He was revealing a Father who cannot bear to see his children suffer the agony of spiritual homelessness. He was revealing a God who longs for restored relationship with humanity.

Being an adopted child has therefore helped me to count my spiritual blessings! I am deeply grateful that my Heavenly Father established an eternal relationship with me, that he adopted me through the saving work of Jesus, and that he gave me his Spirit, the Spirit who enables me to cry out to God, 'Abba! Dear Father!' (Galatians 4:6). It always feels like the most natural thing to thank God for the gift of relationship with him. It is as natural as being grateful to my adoptive parents for their initiative of love.

Physical Blessings

Of all the blessings which we receive, it is probably the ones relating to our spirituality which we most quickly remember. But if these are the only ones which fuel the flames of our thanksgiving, then the chances are we have become a little too spiritual. God's blessings, after all, shower the whole of our lives.

One of the blessings which should promote thanksgiving is the gift of good health. We should never forget to thank God for the fact that our hearts are beating, our lungs are dilating and even for the fact that our bowels are behaving. If we are in good health, we should thank God for it. One day we shall all know what it is like not to be fit.

Connected with this is the blessing of physical healing.

Sometimes God is pleased to heal people physically and this is always a great cause of thanksgiving. I recall a recent incident in which my wife Alie was lying awake in bed, in agony because of a severe viral infection. We had called the doctor and there had been no improvement. Eventually, more in desperation than in faith (though desperation can be a very deep kind of faith), I laid my hands on her and prayed a short and not very believing prayer: 'In the name of Jesus, be healed and sleep well!' Within a few seconds she was asleep. The next morning she was completely healed.

Counting our physical blessings is therefore partly about health and healing. But there are other aspects of our bodies for which we need to give thanks. We need to learn to give thanks for the way God has made us. Our body image should not be influenced by the media's cosmetic understanding of physical shapeliness. Our body image should be influenced by the Word of God. From scriptures like Psalm 139 we need to remember that God designed our bodies in our mothers' wombs. As far as God is concerned, whatever we look like physically, we are fearfully and wonderfully made. God made our bodies and we should therefore thank him for them.

Connected with this is the issue of our sexuality. Again, the biblical expression of our sexuality is something to be enjoyed and celebrated. It is a cause for thanksgiving. Sexual intimacy within marriage is therefore not something shameful, but rather a beautiful and exciting gift of God. If we are blessed enough to be married, let us therefore not hold back from thanking God for the play and intimacy of sexual love. Let us not be Gnostic in our thinking and relegate such matters to the dirty, the ungodly and the evil. Such experiences should form part of the regular repertoire of our gratitude.

In reality, there is an almost limitless potential for thanking the Father when it comes to the physical blessings of life. The following anonymous prayer is a lovely example of someone finding opportunities to be grateful in the things that we so often take for granted all around us:

Lord, I Thank You
Even though I clutch my blanket and growl
when the alarm rings,
thank you, Lord, that I can hear.
There are many who are deaf.

Even though I keep my eyes closed against the morning light
as long as possible,
thank you, Lord, that I can see.
Many are blind.

Even though I huddle in my bed and put off rising,
thank you, Lord, that I have the strength to rise.
There are many who are bedridden.

Even though the first hour of my day is hectic,
when socks are lost,
toast is burned and tempers are short,
my children are so loud,
thank you, Lord, for my family.
There are many who are lonely.

Even though our breakfast table never looks like
the pictures in magazines
and the menu is at times unbalanced,
thank you, Lord, for the food we have.
There are many who are hungry.

Even though the routine of my job
is often monotonous,
thank you, Lord, for the opportunity to work.

Even though I grumble and bemoan my fate
from day to day
and wish my circumstances were not so modest,
thank you, Lord, for life.

I love what Erma Bombeck once said:

An estimated 1.5 million people are living today after bouts
with breast cancer. Every time I forget to feel grateful to be
among them, I hear the voice of an eight-year-old named
Christina, who had cancer of the nervous system.

When asked what she wanted for her birthday, she
thought long and hard and finally said, 'I don't know. I have

two sticker books and a Cabbage Patch doll. I have everything!'

Emotional Blessings

If physical blessings are to be appreciated, so are emotional blessings. Anything which brings joy to our hearts should be the cause
of thanksgiving. The joy of a kiss, the joy of a sunset, the joy of a
compliment, the joy of a child's first steps, the joy of inner healing:
all these can provide us with a heightened sense of gratitude.
Anything that touches, enlivens and blesses our emotions can
become the stimulus for thanksgiving. Anything which helps us to
live life more abundantly, more playfully, more ecstatically, can
make us thankful. Such moments of plenitude can form the content of *berakah* prayer, prayer in which we bless the Lord for his
blessings.

In Chapter 1 I referred to Zechariah, the father of John the
Baptist. It is lovely to note that when his baby boy was eventually
born, he too uttered a *berakah* to God:

> Blessed be the Lord, the God of Israel, because he has come
> and redeemed his people. He has raised up a horn of salvation
> for us in the house of his servant David (as he said through
> his holy prophets of long ago), salvation from our enemies
> and from the hand of all who hate us to show mercy to our
> fathers and to remember his holy covenant, the oath he swore
> to our father Abraham: to rescue us from the hand of our
> enemies and to enable us to serve him without fear in
> holiness and righteousness before him all our days.

At this point, overwhelmed with emotion at the impossible
miracle of his son's birth, Zechariah turns from addressing God to
addressing his baby boy. As a father he starts to prophesy over his
child with absolute delight:

> And you, my child, will be called a prophet of the Most High;
> for you will go on before the Lord to prepare the way for him,
> to give his people the knowledge of salvation through the for-
> giveness of their sins, because of the tender mercy of our
> God, by which the rising sun will come to us from heaven, to

shine on those living in darkness and the shadow of death, to
guide our feet into the path of peace.

Luke 1:68–79

Like Zechariah, we can thank God for emotional blessings.

Intellectual Blessings

The same goes for intellectual blessings. Our minds can be a great
barrier to God but they can also be the locus of tremendous
revelation and pleasure. Those times when we feel as though our
minds have been stimulated, enriched and ennobled are occasions
of thanksgiving, whether the stimulus to that enrichment was a
secular novel or an anointed sermon. Such times should again be
seen as treasures given by the Spirit of God. Thank God for anything that gives you legitimate intellectual stimulation, especially a
good book. As Charles Eliot said in 1896: 'books are the quietest
and most constant of friends; they are the most accessible and wis-
est of counselors, and the most patient of teachers'.

People tend to be, by temperament, either analytical or artistic –
rarely both. When I speak of counting our intellectual blessings I
am thinking of giving thanks for those things which give pleasure
at either the analytical or the artistic level. Those whose thinking is
dominated by mathematical or philosophical leanings may be
blessed by an equation or a maxim. Those whose thinking is dominated by more artistic leanings may derive pleasure from a land-
scape or a poem. 'Whatever is true, whatever is noble, whatever is
right, whatever is pure, whatever is lovely, whatever is admirable –
if anything is excellent or praiseworthy – think about such things'
(Philippians 4:8). Think about them and thank God for them.

Material Blessings

'Take full account of the excellencies which you possess, and in
gratitude remember how you would hanker after them, if you had
them not.' So said Marcus Aurelius Antoninus. We should learn to
thank God for his provision of material and financial blessings. For
most of us, God has provided a roof over our heads and a home for
us to live in. Even if that home will never belong to some of us, we
still have a place to sleep, eat, wash and keep warm in. In a world

where these kinds of things are denied to so many, there is a real need for us to learn gratitude. We must grow to be thankful for toothpaste and toilets, for baths and for basins.

Thanking God for material blessings does not mean advocating what has been called a 'prosperity gospel'. Some Christian leaders in the West are teaching that the blessings given to Abraham, which include material prosperity, can be claimed through faith by today's Christians. I do not concur with that view. Anyone who looks at the life of Jesus and indeed of the first Christians is struck not by a prosperity gospel but by an *austerity* gospel. He or she is struck by the fact of God's gracious provision for our basic needs on the one hand, but also by a call to a simple lifestyle on the other.

This does not, of course, mean an end to feasting and fun. The Christian life involves celebration. That is why Jesus begins his ministry in John's Gospel with the miraculous transformation of about 180 gallons of water into heavenly wine. That signifies to me that the new age of the Spirit, which we are still living in, is an age of joy and festival.

However, the terrible deprivation and degradation of the world's unemployed, hungry, bereaved and destitute will mean that we who bear the name of Christ will also want to set boundaries on spending and feasting. We will want to offer up a constant *berakah* for the way God meets our basic needs, and for those times when he permits us to revel and to play. We will not be a prosperity people but a grateful, disciplined people.

Relational Blessings

Let us remember, finally, to count our relational blessings, the blessings which we receive from our relationships with others. As Albert Schweitzer once said, 'at times our own light goes out and is rekindled by a spark from another person. Each of us has cause to think with deep gratitude of those who have lit the flame within us.'

There are a number of relationships which give me cause for gratitude. First of all, there are those friends who give me the freedom to be myself. In my experience, this is one of the greatest joys: 'to be free to be me'. In my profession as a clergyman, I find that there are many expectations of how I should behave and what I should or should not say. Many of these expectations are right. But the effect of them is that they sometimes force me into a state of unnatural self-vigilance, making it virtually impossible to relax completely. However, the friends who delight in the real me, rather than the professional me, are a real blessing. They are people for whom I give thanks.

Secondly, there are our families. I am blessed to have a wife and four children. My personal testimony is this: that I feel called to offer up a *berakah* for my marriage and my family life *every day*. I feel called to express my gratitude for the relationships within my own home: for the children with their vitality, laughter and health; for my wife, with her beauty, gifts and love. None of them is to be taken for granted. All are a precious gift of God's abundant grace.

Thirdly, there are Christian brothers and sisters whom we meet and with whom, so often, we strike up a mysteriously quick accord. This, like the gift of true friends and family, is also a gift of grace. When Paul says to his Christian brothers and sisters in Philippi, 'I thank my God every time I remember you' (Philippians 1:3), he was speaking with a note of profound gratitude and sincere affection. He was speaking as one who knew the importance of counting relational blessings in prayer. I thank the Father daily for the church I am part of.

Occasions of Thanksgiving

We have looked at spiritual, physical, emotional, intellectual, material and relational blessings. When the Scripture says, 'Out of the fullness of God's grace, God has given us all one blessing after another', these are the kinds of blessings which we need to remember in thankfulness. As Charles Dickens once said, 'reflect upon your present blessings, of which every man has plenty; not on your past misfortunes of which all men have some'.

There is always something that you and I can give thanks to the Father for. The Scottish minister Alexander Whyte was famous for his prayers before preaching. He always found something for which to be thankful to God. One Sunday morning the weather was so awful that one member of the church thought, 'The minister will never think of anything for which to thank God on a day like this.' Much to his surprise, however, Whyte began by praying, 'We thank Thee, O God, that it is not always like this.'

How much time, then, should be spent on such thanksgiving?

On a daily basis, between two and ten minutes should be adequate. This is simply because the amount of time we are reviewing is usually limited to 24 hours. Usually we will be looking back over the previous day and night, so the amount for which we can give thanks is finite. However, there are some occasions in the year when it is good to spend much longer in thanksgiving, indeed when it is right to spend the majority of time giving thanks.

Longer periods of thanksgiving are important at the end of every week. On our birthday it is good to look back over the whole year. The same is true for a wedding anniversary, or for New Year's Eve. Do not forget your spiritual birthday either: if you know the date when you were converted, use that day as a day of thanksgiving. Thank God for leading you to where you are right now.

There are consequently some set occasions for a special ministry of thanksgiving. The most important occasions of all, however, are not anniversaries but seasons of tribulation or dryness. I honestly believe that the ability to thank God for some of the negative experiences of our lives is as important, if not more important, than the ability to thank him for all the positive things which we have discussed so far. It is easy to thank God when the going is easy. It is much harder, of course, when we are under stress. But the ability to thank God in the hard times is actually a deep sign of trust. It is the true measure of spiritual maturity.

The basis for gratitude in adverse circumstances is the fact that God is sovereign, and so all things ultimately work to the good for those who love him. Thanking God when times are hard is a sure sign that we trust that '*Everything* that God does, he does for a purpose.' With that in mind, we can more easily obey Paul when he writes, 'Give thanks (*eucharisteite*) in all circumstances, for this is God's will for you in Christ Jesus' (1 Thessalonians 5:18). Though this can be extremely tough, it releases great rewards to those who persevere.

One man who took this principle to heart was the German pastor Martin Rinkart who, in 1636, after burying 5,000 of his parishioners during one year of the plague, sat down and wrote a grace for his children to say before their meal:

> Now thank we all our God
> With heart and hands and voices;
> Who wondrous things hath done,

In whom His world rejoices.
Who, from our mother's arms,
Hath led us on our way
With countless gifts of love
And still is ours today.

There was a man who knew how to thank God, even in the most desperately adverse circumstances. As Leroy Paige once said, 'don't pray when it rains if you don't pray when the sun shines'.

One of Our Best Words

As a father of four children, I have found over the years that spontaneous gratitude is one of the greatest gifts a child can give to their parents. When I freely choose to take my children out for a treat, or give them an unexpected gift, my children tend to say thank you. When this thanksgiving is uttered entirely spontaneously, without any coaxing from their Mum, it thrills my heart. Hearing those simple words, 'thanks Dad', are indescribably uplifting. In fact, when they are uttered spontaneously, they have the effect of making me want to be even more generous! They enlarge my heart with an even greater desire to bless my children. Gratitude is quite simply irresistible to me as a father. And it is irresistible to God the Father too. As the Perfect Father, he is profoundly affected by our simple words of thanksgiving. Saying 'thanks' to God causes his heart to increase too. Our gratitude attracts more of his goodness. And so the process goes on and on.

So we should not underestimate the power of gratitude. The Message version of Psalm 100:4 says, 'enter with the password: "Thank you!"' I love that. All we need to do to access the Father's presence is simply say 'thanks'. That's the password that opens the door into his courts.

It is said that when Rudyard Kipling was writing at his prime, he received a shilling for every word that he wrote for one particular newspaper. Some undergraduates at Oxford University heard about this and, as a ruse, sent Kipling a shilling, and asked him to send them one of his best words. Immediately Kipling cabled back a one-word answer to the students: 'Thanks!'

'Thanks' is one of our best words as Christians.

Prayer

Dear Father, I want now to enter your gates with thanksgiving. Please lead me, as a priest of your Kingdom, into an authentic eucharistic ministry. Help me to overflow with thankfulness.

I want to begin by thanking you that out of the fullness of your grace, you have given me one blessing after another. Help me now to count my beads of gracious moments. Help me to savour all those ways in which you have helped me to enjoy life in all its fullness.

Lord, I thank you for the following spiritual blessings over the last 24 hours . . .

Lord, I thank you for all the physical blessings too . . .

Thank you for those moments when you have touched my emotions . . .

Thank you for the following material blessings . . .

Thank you for feeding my mind . . .

And thank you for the relationships which I have been privileged to enjoy since we last met in this way . . .

Thank you, Father. Amen.

THREE

The Court of Praise

Man need never be so defeated that he cannot do anything. Weak, sick, broken in body, far from home, and alone in a strange land, he can sing! He can worship!
Ernest Gordon, *Miracle on the River Kwai*

The first stage of prayer is now complete. We have looked back over the time since we last prayed, and given voice to our gratitude for what the Father has done for us. As we have done so, the gates of his holy presence have opened wide, revealing the inner court in which the great sanctuary was situated. This is the court of praise. It is a place of adoration.

Before we examine the actual practice of praise, we need to look in more detail at this inner court. According to most scholars there were two main courts in the Temple area. There was first of all the outer court, sometimes called the court of the Gentiles. This area, paved with flagstones and mosaics, could be entered by anyone. A little to the west was a stairway which you had to climb in order to reach the terrace on which the sanctuary was built. This raised area was an inner court also known as the court of the priests. Whereas anyone could enter the court of the Gentiles, only priests could climb the stairway and enter the raised inner court.

It is this raised inner court of which the psalmist often speaks. It is this area of the Temple for which he longs with all his heart:

> My soul yearns, even faints,
> for the courts of the Lord;
> my heart and my flesh cry out
> for the living God.
> Even the sparrow has found a home,
> and the swallow a nest for herself,
> where she may have her young –
> a place near your altar,
> O LORD Almighty, my King and my God.
>
> Psalm 84:2–4

The reason why the psalmist longs to be in this upper court is because it is the place of ongoing praise and adoration of God. So when the writer of Psalm 100 says, 'Enter his gates with thanksgiving and his courts with praise', we can understand him to be asking the people of God to spend time not only thanking God for what he has done, but also to proceed beyond that, to a higher level of worship, in which heartfelt praise is offered for God's infinite and unfathomable nature.

The Challenge of Praise

In the last chapter I mentioned the common distinction between thanksgiving and praise. Thanksgiving is about God's acts. Praise is about God's being. In thanksgiving we express our gratitude for what God has done for us. In praising God we worship him simply for who he is.

This distinction is important in practice. My experience of open prayer suggests that we are much better at thanking God than we are at praising him. Whenever a leader says, 'Let's praise God', it is amazing how often what follows is, in reality, thanksgiving. We launch with enthusiasm and eloquence into thanking God for the Cross, for healing, for answered prayer, and so on. In the process, we do not realise that, strictly speaking, we have mis-understood the directive. The leader said, 'Let us praise!' not 'Let us thank!'

One of the reasons why we find it so hard to praise is because of the limitations of our language. Deep down we recognise that our finite vocabulary is insufficient to describe God's infinite nature. So when we are urged to praise God, we all of us hesitate and feel a bit lost. How on earth are we going to find the words to express sincere awe at a God who is in heaven? How are we going to praise him without either sounding pious or superficial? At least in the area of thanksgiving we are dealing with things that we can see and touch. But with praise, that is a different matter altogether. Here we are attempting to bridge that enormous, metaphysical gap between ourselves and the One who is immortal and invisible. Here we are attempting to put into words things that almost feel indescribable.

One reason behind the poverty of our praise in public worship lies with our vocabulary. Another has to do with our own, personal prayer life. The fact is that the corporate is always an expression of the private. Put another way, how we pray in public is a very good indication of how we pray on our own. One of the main reasons for the poverty of praise in public has to do with a poverty of praise in our private devotion. For many of us it is true to say that our prayer life is far more preoccupied with who we are than who God is. Far more time is given to confession, often with a suggestion of negative self-absorption, than to adoration.

The Importance of Praise

Praise is, quite simply, vital. It is vital, first of all, to the Father. Our Heavenly Father loves to hear us praise him for specific aspects of his character. He does not love to hear our praise for the reasons we love praise. In other words, he does not crave adoration because his ego needs boosting, or because his heart needs affirming. The Father has no such unmet needs or insecurities. He loves to hear our praise because it shows him that we desire to understand and value him, however far short of total comprehension this will inevitably fall.

To illustrate this, look at the analogy of human relationships. If you were to ask my wife Alie which she preferred, thanksgiving or praise, she would probably reply, 'I like both, but I prefer being praised.' If I say, 'Thank you for that lovely meal,' that gives Alie pleasure because it shows her that I have not taken her hard work for granted. But if I say, 'Alie, I think you're the most creative person I know,' that gives her even greater pleasure. It shows her that I love her for who she is, and not for what she does for me. So it is with God. C. S. Lewis put it this way:

> I think we delight to praise what we enjoy because the praise not merely expresses but completes the enjoyment. It is not out of compliment that lovers keep on telling one another how beautiful they are; the delight is incomplete till it is expressed.

The Father loves to hear us praise him for all the multi-faceted qualities of his character. He longs to know that we love him for who he is and not for what we can get out of him. Too many relationships today are the product of 'utilitarian individualism'. In other words, they exist because we can get something out of the other person. This is not to be true of our relationship with God. God is not a 'credit card deity' whom we can access for our own needs. He is the One, True Living God in whom we live and move and have our being. A healthy diet of praise each day keeps us from appreciating our Father only for what he gives us.

The Benefits of Praise

If praise is important to our Father, it is also important to us. Our spiritual health depends largely upon us spending time each day gazing with devotion upon God's being. Put another way, the practice of praising our Father is good for our spiritual, emotional and physical well being.

This came home to me with particular force when I was asked to minister to a man who was suffering from depression. He had received a lot of counselling but it produced little fruit. When I started helping him I had no idea what to do but I did feel burdened to take him back to basics: I began to re-lay the foundations of his faith by talking about the essentials of discipleship and by gently challenging him on each of these.

Not surprisingly, this did not help very much. It drove him deeper into guilt and left me with the distinct impression that we were getting nowhere. However, one day we had a breakthrough. Unplanned by me, we started looking at aspects of God's nature, focusing initially upon his fatherly love, then upon his holiness, and so on. As soon as this happened, my friend's eyes lit up. He seemed to come alive. Indeed, I can remember his words: 'Now *this* is really helpful. It's a lot more healthy concentrating upon God than upon me. Let's run with this approach for a while. I need to judge my circumstances in the light of God, not God in the light of my circumstances.'

What the Father was teaching me was the healing power of praise. Through praise, we stop staring downwards at the shadow of our hurts and sins (which are enough to depress many of us) and we start to look upwards at a much more soul-affirming reality, the beauty of the Father-heart of God. As Teresa of Avila once put it:

> Self-knowledge is necessary, no matter how high the state of the soul, and we must never neglect it. Humility must ever be doing its work like a bee making honey in the hive; without humility all is lost. But sometimes the soul must emerge from self-knowledge and soar aloft in meditation on the greatness

and majesty of its God. Thus it will realize its own baseness rather than in thinking about itself. *We shall reach much greater heights of virtue by thinking of the virtue of God than if we stay in our own little plot of ground and tie ourselves down to it completely* [my italics].[1]

One person who discovered this truth and expressed it with conviction was the poet John Milton. He was a man who had good cause for introspection and depression. He went blind, a severe handicap to a man who dearly wanted to serve God as a poet. One of his most poignant poems is about his spiritual journey from confusion to acceptance. It is simply called, 'On his blindness'.

Milton's poem is a sonnet. A sonnet is a carefully constructed poem of fourteen lines, in which very often the first eight lines portray a problem, and the final six lines present some kind of solution, usually beginning with the word 'but'. Milton's is no exception. In the first eight lines, he laments the loss of his sight before he is halfway through the course of his life. He laments that his eyesight is now hidden, like a talent, and that his eyes are now lodged in their sockets as useless organs:

> When *I* consider how *my* light is spent
> Ere half *my* days, in this dark world and wide,
> And that one talent which is death to hide,
> Lodg'd with *me* useless, though *my* soul more bent
> To serve therewith *my* Maker, and present
> *My* true account, lest he returning chide;
> 'Doth God exact day-labour, light denied,'
> *I* fondly ask . . .

In these eight lines, the most noticeable feature of the language is the emphasis upon the self. I have put all the first-person pronouns in italics so as to highlight the degree of self-preoccupation and self-doubt which Milton clearly felt. What is so striking in the second half of the poem is the transition from 'self-centred' language to 'God-centred' language. The way out of Milton's depression occurs when he moves from an emphasis upon 'me' to an emphasis upon 'him' (i.e. God). As is so often the case, the word 'but' marks the transition:

But Patience, to prevent
That murmur, soon replies, '*God* doth not need
Either man's work, or *his* own gifts; who best
Bear *his* mild yoke, they serve *him* best: *his* state
Is kingly; thousands at *his* bidding speed,
And post o'er land and ocean without rest;
They also serve who only stand and wait.

Milton's sonnet is a testimony to emotional healing. In the first eight lines he is preoccupied with himself and with his blindness. In the second part of the poem he decides to become preoccupied with God. Instead of going deeper into himself, Milton chooses to dwell upon God's goodness. From the eighth line onwards, there are therefore no more references to 'I', to 'me', but only to 'God', to 'him', to 'he'. This enables Milton to close his sonnet with a beautiful statement of assurance. Having focused upon God's 'kingly state', he declares that 'They also serve who only stand and wait.' Even those whose disabilities necessitate a more passive role are authentic servants of God.

This poem is a beautiful example of the way in which the power of praise can liberate us from toxic introspection. As C. S. Lewis once put it, 'Praise almost seems to be inner health made audible.' Praise is the audible consequence of a soul whose gaze is turned upwards rather than inwards.

The Practice of Praise

Given the poverty of our language, how can we best praise God? The first thing to realise is that God has given us a wonderful thesaurus of praise in the Scriptures where he has taken hold of our frail and finite vocabulary and invested it with a capacity for true revelation. One of the ways through the language barrier is to take hold of the Scriptures which are adorational in character and to use them as the basis of our own worship.

The Psalms are a particularly helpful resource in this respect. These songs are, in all probability, the hymns which were sung in the Temple. The praise psalms are divided into those which are descriptive and those which are declarative. The descriptive psalms describe the great things which God has done while the declarative psalms tend to rejoice in who God is. The descriptive psalms are therefore an aid to thanksgiving (which addresses God's deeds) while the declarative psalms are an aid to praise (which addresses God's being). One example of a declarative psalm is Psalm 30:4–5:

> Sing to the LORD, you saints of his;
> praise his holy name.
> For his anger lasts only a moment,
> but his favour lasts a lifetime;
> Weeping may return for a night,
> but rejoicing comes in the morning!

Notice the words 'anger' and 'favour', which perfectly capture those two aspects of God's nature which we often describe as 'justice' and 'love'. 'Anger' and 'favour' are beautiful synonyms for 'justice' and 'love'. They could easily form the basis of personal praise:

> O Lord God, I praise you for your holy anger, a side of your nature I often choose to neglect. I praise you that you are holy, that you are justly angered by my sins. But I praise you even more because your anger lasts only a moment, while your favour lasts a lifetime. Praise you for your kindness, your mercy and your favour, Lord.

This practice of praying back the Scriptures which are adorational in character is one of the most powerful spiritual disciplines, both in private and public prayer. Too often we treat Scripture as information when it is often declaration. The devotional exclamations of the Psalms can bring great blessing to our spirit if we turn them back into that purpose for which many of them were originally designed: devotion.

One emphasis which we often find in the Psalms is on the name of the Lord. Praising the Lord for his 'name' is a frequent characteristic of the declarative psalms. The psalm which we have just examined exhorts us to 'praise his holy name' (30:4). The greatest of these names is 'Jehovah' or 'Yahweh', which David Pawson has translated as 'Always'. This translation helps us to use God's name in personal praise:

> Jehovah Roi – Always my Shepherd
> Jehovah Jireh – Always my Provider
> Jehovah Nissi – Always my Banner
> Jehovah Shalom – Always my Peace
> Jehovah Shammah – Always There
> Jehovah Tsidkenu – Always my Righteousness
> Jehovah M'Kaddesh – Always my Holiness
> Jehovah Rapha – Always my Healer

The thing to remember about these names is that the word 'Jehovah' comes from a root that suggests a continual state of existence. As we praise God, we can worship him for the fact that God has never stopped being all the things above, and always will be. No wonder the psalmist tells us to praise God's holy name (30:4; 69:30; 96:2; 145:21; 148:13).

Jesus Christ, Lord of All

If it is important to praise the name of the Lord using the Old Testament Scriptures, how much more important it is to praise him using the language of the New Testament. In the New Testament there are many new names or titles given to Jesus, the Son of God. I have found it very helpful to take these names and to use them in what I call 'the praise of high Christology'.

What then is high Christology? Christology is our understanding of the person and significance of Jesus Christ. All of us, as Christians, have a Christology. Revisionist Christians tend to have a 'low' Christology, an understanding of Jesus as a moral teacher, the embodiment of love, a window on to God. Such phrases stop far short of saying that Jesus was the unique Son of God, the Messiah, the Risen and Ascended Lord. This second kind of understanding is usually embraced by more orthodox Christians, especially those who believe that the Bible is the Word of God. This second position would be termed a 'high Christology'.

My personal conviction is that a high Christology is the only Christology which makes sense of the biblical evidence and of the Church's experience of Jesus. Marcus Borg, a fine New Testament scholar, has recently written a widely acclaimed work entitled *Jesus. A New Vision*, which begins with these powerful words about the impact and status of Jesus of Nazareth:

No other figure in the history of the West has ever been accorded such extraordinary status. Within a few decades of his death, stories were told of his miraculous birth. By the end of the first century, he was extolled with the most exalted titles known within the religious tradition out of which he came: Son of God, one with the Father, the Word become flesh, the bread of life, the light of the world, the one who would come again as cosmic judge and Lord. Within a few centuries he had become Lord of the empire which had crucified him.

As if this was not impressive enough, Borg goes on to highlight the towering supremacy and influence of Jesus on the rest of history:

For over a thousand years thereafter, he dominated the culture of the West: its religion and devotion, its art, music, and architecture, its intellectual thought and ethical norms, even its politics. Our calendar affirms his life as a dividing point in world history. On historical grounds alone, with no convictions of faith shaping the verdict, Jesus is the most important figure in Western (and perhaps human) history.[2]

These words show from the evidence of history that Jesus is worthy of the highest honour. Combine this with the evidence of Scripture, and the evidence of our personal experience, and we have good grounds for celebrating the ultimacy of Jesus. 'High Christology' should therefore form the true content of our praise in the court of the priests!

One reason why this is so important is because there has been a slow and destructive erosion of high Christology over the course of the last hundred years or so. Two factors in particular have contributed to this.

First of all, it cannot be denied that liberal theology has significantly influenced the widespread loss of nerve concerning the deity of Jesus. Many scholars argued that this belief was written into the Gospels by the early Church. Rudolf Bultmann, who claimed that all high Christology is redactional (i.e. superimposed on to the teaching of the historical Jesus), is perhaps the most famous example of this position.

The ramifications of this scholarship for the life of the Church should not be ignored. Many people training in theological and Bible colleges since the Second World War have been exposed to this hermeneutic of scepticism. This has produced a generation of ministers who have adopted a liberal perspective on Jesus. Even bishops have publicly stated that the virgin birth of Jesus was invented by the early Church, and that one can no longer be certain about anything which the New Testament says.

Theological liberalism has therefore produced a portrait of Jesus in which the elements pertaining to his uniqueness and his deity have been stripped away. But there has been a second cause for concern as well. This second corrosive factor has been the emergence of a confusing religious pluralism. There are many religious cults today which masquerade as Christian and yet which contain a very low Christology at best, and at worst a view of Jesus based on nothing short of deception. These movements are also influencing the Church, the academic world and society as a whole. Most obvious are the large number of religious beliefs which have been subsumed under the label, the New Age. It is difficult to talk precisely about such an amorphous movement, but one common denominator seems to be a highly deceptive and erroneous view of Jesus. On the surface of it, New Agers appear to have the highest of all christologies. They speak of the Christ Spirit, and of the Cosmic Christ who pervades the universe. However, close inspection reveals that this is just a cover-up for a very destructive view of Jesus.

The two streams of liberalism and pluralism have contributed to a gradual sense of uncertainty about Jesus in many believers. This stands to reason if we think about it for a moment: how can we worship Jesus as the Lord of all when modern trends of thought are arguing that he was never Lord at all?

Recovering the Ground

One way of regaining confidence is by praying back to God those scriptures which use exalted names and titles for Jesus. Biblical passages which contain a high Christology can legitimately form the content of our praise in the courts of praise. Peter, in his first letter, commands us, 'in your hearts, set apart Christ as Lord' (1 Peter 3:15); in other words, 'Develop the regular discipline of exalting Jesus with heartfelt praise.' He then goes on to add, 'Always be prepared to give an answer to everyone who asks you to give the reason for the hope that you have' (1 Peter 3:15).

The second of these statements, 'Always be ready to give a defence', and the first of these statements, 'Set apart Christ as Lord', are not unconnected remarks: they are logically related. Indeed, the first command constitutes a cause, the second its effect. The more we set apart Christ as Lord in our hearts (through prayers of praise), the more ready we shall be to provide a reasoned and cogent defence of our hope (through evangelism). The more we fill our hearts with praise for the Lord Jesus, the more fluently our mouths will utter truths concerning the ultimacy of the Lord Jesus.

There are many names and titles for Jesus in the New Testament. I find it helpful to pray using an A to Z of his names. This is a practice which has quite a history in evangelical circles and is, I believe, enormously beneficial.[3] Many people have remarked to me how the A to Z of Jesus' names has given them a whole new lease of life in the court of praise.

The following is an A to Z of Jesus' New Testament names which can be used in the court of praise.

A   Advocate with the Father (1 John 2:1)
      Alpha (Revelation 22:13)
      The Amen (Revelation 3:14)
      Apostle whom we Confess (Hebrews 3:1)
      The Atoning Sacrifice (1 John 2:2)
      Author of Life (Acts 3:15)
      Author of Our Salvation (Hebrews 2:10)
      Author of Our Faith (Hebrews 12:2)

B   Beginning (Revelation 22:13)
      Beloved (Ephesians 1:6)
      Beloved Son (Matthew 3:17)
      Blameless One (Hebrews 7:26)
      Bread of God (John 6:33)
      Bread of Life (John 6:35)
      Bridegroom (John 3:29)
      Bright Morning Star (Revelation 22:16)

C   Capstone (1 Peter 2:7)
Chief Cornerstone (Ephesians 2:20; 1 Peter 2:6)
Chief Shepherd (1 Peter 5:4)
Chosen by God (1 Peter 2:4)
Christ
The Christ
The Christ of God
Christ Jesus
Christ Jesus the Lord
Christ the Lord
Christ our Passover Lamb (1 Corinthians 5:7)
Consolation of Israel (Luke 2:25)

D   Descendant of David (Romans 1:3)
Door of the Sheep (John 10:7)

E   Emmanuel (Matthew 1:23)
Eternal Life (1 John 5:20)
Exact Representation of God (Hebrews 1:3)
Exalted above the Heavens (Hebrews 7:26)

F   Faithful (1 Thessalonians 5:24)
Faithful and True (Revelation 19:11)
Faithful Witness (literally 'Martyr': Revelation 1:5)
Faithful High Priest (Hebrews 2:17)
First (Revelation 22:13)
Firstborn (Hebrews 1:6; 12:23)
Firstborn among many Brothers (Romans 8:29)
Firstborn from the Dead (Revelation 1:5)
Firstborn over all Creation (Colossians 1:15)
First Fruits of those who have Fallen Asleep (1 Corinthians 15:20)
Foundation (1 Corinthians 3:11)
Fragrant Offering (Ephesians 5:2)
Friend of Sinners (Luke 7:34)

G   Glory of the One and Only (John 1:14)
God Over All (Romans 8:5)
God With Us (Matthew 1:23)
Good Shepherd (John 10:11)

Great God (Titus 2:13)
Great High Priest (Hebrews 4:14)
Great Shepherd of the Sheep (Hebrews 13:20)
Greater than Abraham (John 8:53)
Greater than Jacob (John 4:12)
Greater than Jonah (Matthew 12:41)
Greater than Solomon (Matthew 12:42)
Greater than the Temple (Matthew 12:6)

H Head over Every Power and Authority (Colossians 2:10)
Head of Every Man (1 Corinthians 11:3)
Head of the Body, the Church (Colossians 1:18)
Heir of All Things (Hebrews 1:2)
High Priest (Hebrews 5:5)
High Priest after the Order of Melchizedek (Hebrews 5:10)
High Priest forever (Hebrews 6:20)
Holy One (Acts 2:27)
Holy One of God (John 6:69)
Holy and Righteous One (Acts 3:14)
Holy Servant (Acts 4:27)
Our Hope (1 Timothy 1:1)
Hope of Glory (Colossians 1:27)
Hope of Israel (Acts 28:20)
Horn of Salvation (Luke 1:69)

I I Am (John 8:28)
Image of the Invisible God (Colossians 1:15)
The Innocent One (Matthew 12:7)

J Jesus
Jesus Christ
Jesus Christ the Lord
Jesus Christ, the Son of God
Jesus of Galilee
Jesus of Nazareth
Judge of the Living and the Dead (Acts 10:42)

K Kindness and Love of God (Titus 3:4)
King of Israel (John 1:49)
King of Kings (Revelation 19:16)

King of Peace (Hebrews 7:2)
King of Righteousness (Hebrews 7:2)

L   Lamb (Revelation 17:14)
     Lamb of God (John 1:29)
     Lamb that was Slain from the Creation of the World
     (Revelation 13:8)
     The Lamb who was Slain (Revelation 5:12)
     Last (Revelation 22:13)
     The Last Adam (1 Corinthians 15:45)
     Life (John 14:6)
     Light (John 1:7)
     Light of Men (John 1:4)
     Light of the World (John 8:12)
     Light for Revelation to the Gentiles (Luke 2:32)
     Lion of Judah (Revelation 5:5)
     Living Bread (John 6:51)
     Lord
     Lord of the Sabbath (Mark 2:28)
     Lord and Saviour (2 Peter 1:11)
     Lord of Both the Dead and the Living (Romans 14:9)
     The Lord of Glory (1 Corinthians 2:8)
     Lord of Lords (Revelation 19:16)

M   Man (Behold the Man! John 19:5)
     A Man Accredited by God (Acts 2:22)
     The Man Christ Jesus (1 Timothy 2:5)
     The Man God has Appointed (Acts 17:31)
     Mediator (1 Timothy 2:5)
     Mediator of a new covenant (Hebrews 12:24)
     Merciful (Hebrews 2:17)
     Morning Star (2 Peter 1:19)
     Mystery of God (Colossians 2:2)

N   Name Above Every Name (Philippians 2:9)

O   Offering (Ephesians 5:2)
     Offspring of David (Revelation 22:16)
     Omega (Revelation 22:13)
     The One and Only (John 1:14, 3:16)

P   Our Peace (Ephesians 2:14)
Perfecter of Our Faith (Hebrews 12:2)
Power of God (1 Corinthians 1:24)
Prince and Saviour (Acts 5:31)
Prophet, Powerful in Word and Deed (Luke 24:19)

R   Radiance of God's Glory (Hebrews 1:3)
Ransom for All Men (1 Timothy 2:6)
Ransom for Many (Mark 10:45)
Redemption (1 Corinthians 1:30)
Resurrection (John 11:25)
Righteous Judge (2 Timothy 4:8)
Righteous One (Acts 7:52; 1 John 2:1)
Rising Sun (Luke 1:78)
Root of David (Revelation 5:5)
Ruler of the Kings of the Earth (Revelation 1:5)

S   Sacrifice to God (Ephesians 5:2)
Salvation (Luke 2:30)
Saviour (Titus 2:13)
Saviour of the Body, the Church (Ephesians 5:10)
Saviour of the World (John 4:42)
Second Adam (1 Corinthians 15:46–7)
Shepherd and Overseer of our Souls (1 Peter 2:25)
The Son
Son of Abraham (Matthew 1:1)
Son of Adam (Luke 3:38)
Son of the Blessed One (Mark 14:61)
Son of David (Matthew 1:1)
Son of the Father (2 John 3)
Son of God
Son of the Living God (Matthew 16:16)
Son of Man
Son of the Most High (Luke 1:32)
Supreme (Colossians 1:18)

T   Teacher Come from God (John 3:2)
True Vine (John 15:1)
The Truth (John 14:6)

U   Unknown God (Acts 17:23)

V   Vine (John 15:1)

W   Way (John 14:6)
     Wisdom of God (1 Corinthians 1:24)
     The Word (John 1:1)
     The Word of Life (1 John 1:1)
     The Worthy One (Revelation 5:12)

Y   The Yes of God (2 Corinthians 1:18–20)

Using the Names in Prayer

There are really three ways of using this A to Z of Christology. First of all, you can meditate on one name and worship Jesus using that. For example, today I concentrated on Jesus as 'The One and Only of God'. Having done a bit of research using the commentaries, I discovered that the Greek word translated 'One and Only' is *monogenes*. This means 'of a single (*monos*) kind (*genos*)' or 'unique'. This in turn is almost certainly a Greek form of the Hebrew word *yahid* meaning 'only, precious', a word used in Genesis 22:2, 12, 16 of Abraham's son Isaac ('your son, your only son').

With that piece of information in my mind I turned to the three New Testament texts which use this description of Jesus:

> We have seen his glory, the glory of the One and Only, who came from the Father, full of grace and truth (John 1:14).

> No one has ever seen God, but God the One and Only, who is at the Father's side, has made him known (John 1:18).

> For God so loved the world that he gave his One and Only Son, that whoever believes in him shall not perish but have eternal life (John 3:16).

Using the language of these verses, I was able to praise Jesus for the fact that he is the One and Only One, the unique and infinitely precious Son of God, who is full of glory, grace, truth, revelation and life. Using just one of the many titles in the A to Z above, I was able to soar to new heights in prayers of praise.

The second way of praising Jesus is either to take all the titles under one letter and pray through those, or to take one title from each letter and just start with A and proceed to Z. However, you may have to do some research concerning the full significance of some of these descriptive names if they are to yield their true significance. The example above ('One and Only') shows that there are great depths in many of these christological expressions.

The third way of using this list involves praying to God those names for Jesus which have greatest relevance to the Temple. There is much in the letter to the Hebrews which helps us to worship Jesus in language reminiscent of the Temple. Why not try using Hebrews 4:14—5:10 as your principal resource for praise? These magnificent words describe Jesus as the Great High Priest who has gone through the heavens, who is able to sympathise with our weaknesses, who has opened up the way to God's throne, who was anointed high priest by God himself, high priest in the order of Melchizedek. You can also use Hebrews 7:11—10:18 in a similar way to praise Jesus for having opened up the sanctuary of heaven, and for having given you access to the most holy place of God's presence. These chapters are among the most worshipful in the entire Bible.

The Prayer of the Mind

So what are the virtues of this kind of praise? First of all, this kind of praise is *biblical*. Recently a number of prominent Christian writers have been complaining that the evangelical world has lost a sense of its roots in the area of spirituality. As the description above should have demonstrated, using the names of Jesus is a true evangelical discipline, drawing from the well of Scripture.

Secondly, this kind of praise is *theological*, it is prayer 'with the mind'. Paul reminds us of the need to engage our mental faculties in worship when he writes: 'I will pray with my spirit but I will also pray with my mind; I will sing with my spirit but I will also sing with my mind' (1 Corinthians 14:15). One of the virtues of using the praise of high Christology is that it does make our prayer life more theologically rich. This kind of praise renews the mind.

This is vital. It was Karl Barth who often said that theology should become more prayerful.[4] For this reason, Barth insisted that students should do their theological reflection with a window open to the heavens! He also pointed to Anselm's *Proslogion*, a great theological work couched entirely in the form of worshipful prayer. For Barth, the *Proslogion* represented the purest form of theological expression. But the converse is also true. Just as theology needs to become more prayerful, so prayer needs to become more theological. In ministering to God in the court of praise we need to use the rich resources of Scripture in order to worship God with our minds. We need to be as theological (certainly as christological) as possible.

A third virtue in this kind of praise is that it is *practical*. By this I mean that it has consequences for evangelism. The discipline of using Christology in prayer functions like a branding iron, burning the ultimacy of Jesus into the thick hide of our lives. By constantly rehearsing the grounds of high Christology in prayer, we make our belief in the deity of Jesus one of the pillars of our spirituality. In the process we find that giving a defence for our hope in Jesus Christ (1 Peter 3:15) becomes more natural.

These, then, are just three of the main reasons why the prayer of high Christology is a virtuous, soul-affirming discipline. They show how important it is to go on from the gates of thanksgiving to the second stage in the Temple of God's presence. Here we spend time in the court of praise, praising God for his name. This involves engaging the mind in prayer.

The Prayer of the Heart

Having said all that, I have to confess that there are days when I do not use this form of praise. There are days when I simply bow before the Father and say, like a little child, 'I love you. You are my Lord and my God. You are my Father and my Friend. I love you Lord.' This kind of praise I call 'the prayer of the heart'. It is a valid and invaluable form of praise. Indeed, God commands us to love him with all of our heart as well as with all our mind. Loving him with the whole of my mind is what the prayer of high Christology is about; but sometimes even this can feel inappropriate, and all that is needed on my part is a simple 'I love you, Father.'

However, some readers may find this difficult. The ability to say

'I love you' to our Father in heaven will not come easily to those of us whose own childhood was not marked by physical affection and open declarations of love. This has been partly true for me. My family upbringing was not characterised by overt displays of love. The reason for that was because my own parents were themselves brought up on a model of family which was rooted in middle-class respectability and the repression of feelings. Consequently, in their parenting of me, my father and mother merely repeated a pattern which was almost certainly multi-generational.

But I recall a day some time ago when my father was staying not far from where I live. I felt a strong leading of the Spirit to go over to where he was and to tell him simply that I loved him. This was perhaps one of the hardest things I have ever done. I was terribly frightened of embarrassment or rejection. But when the moment came, my father put his arms around me, held me, and said, 'I love you too.' It was an utterly transforming moment. From that time on, affection became natural. The years of tactile deprivation disappeared like a mist.

The prayer of the heart is prayer in which our feelings of love towards the Father are released from our fragile hearts. It is a simple 'I love you' to God. One such prayer from the heart can be worth a hundred prayers from the mind.

The Prayer of the Spirit

What goes for the heart also goes for the spirit. Sometimes it will seem good to us and to the Holy Spirit neither to pray with the mind nor even to pray from the heart like a child. Sometimes we are simply moved by the Holy Spirit into the language of the Spirit, the edifying and adorational use of the gift of tongues.

The gift of tongues, we should remember, is a ground-to-air phenomenon. It is prayer uttered by my spirit, prompted by the Holy Spirit, and directed heavenwards towards the throne. In this respect it differs from the gift of prophecy. Prophecy is an air-to-ground phenomenon. It is the revelation of the mind of Christ, through the Holy Spirit, to believers on the earth.

In the court of praise it is sometimes fitting and right to stand in awe of God and to be led by the Spirit into operating in this gift. Now obviously there are Christians who do not speak in tongues. If you are one of those, please do not feel excluded by these words.

Do not feel that your prayer life is any the less valid because of that. But at the same time, please appreciate the importance of tongues for others. One of its greatest virtues is that it helps people to overcome the problem of language which I mentioned at the start of this chapter. Praising God in tongues is the irrational language of an ecstatic spirit. It is worship that transcends words, and in that respect it is infinitely precious.

The prayer of the spirit is therefore a valid and edifying medium of praise.

Mind, Heart and Spirit

Of course, in practice this division of mind, heart and spirit can prove to be artificial. At its best, praise involves all three dimensions of our being – our thinking, our feelings and our spirits. To illustrate this, look at these words written by a busy housewife, after she had heard me speak not long ago about the gates of thanksgiving and the court of praise:

> In our bedroom I have a little table which I use as an altar. I lit my three candles and switched off all the lights and knelt, gazing up at the palm cross on the wall. The stillness and the candles helped me to remember that I'd come to thank and praise God and so I began. The amazing thing about thanksgiving is that you begin to realise just how many times God has blessed your life. You could spend hours on thanksgiving alone. I moved on into praise and decided to sing. I'd got a copy of *Mission Praise* and casually flipped over pages, looking for hymns of praise that I knew. Some of the ones I didn't know seemed to have such powerful words that I made up tunes as I went along. This became quite enjoyable and I must have spent 20 minutes or so picking out hymns which expressed how I felt. Then came the tongues. I like singing in tongues. Somehow, the sounds and 'words' remind me of the prayers chanted by the Jewish priests. It makes me feel special. No one knows what I am saying to God, it's so private and intimate. As I sang, new 'words' entered the language, which surprised me and one of them was the name 'Jesu'. I realised that my focus was changing and then slowly, gradually, there were just two sounds left, one of them being 'Jesu'.

I found that an incredible feeling of peace was now surrounding me and I felt physically held, as though arms were supporting me and holding me still.

At its best, our worship involves the whole person. No one has put it better than former Archbishop William Temple:

> Worship is the submission of all our nature to God. It is the quickening of conscience by His holiness; the nourishment of mind with His truth; the purifying of imagination by His beauty; the opening of the heart to His love; the surrender of will to His purpose – and all of this gathered up in adoration, the most selfless emotion of which our nature is capable and therefore the chief remedy for that self-centredness which is our original sin and the source of all actual sin.

The Sacrifice of Praise

In conclusion, we do need to recognise that praising God requires sacrifice on our part. Perhaps that is why we are called to love God not only with all our mind, heart and soul, but also with all our strength. Praise requires a strong sacrifice of the will in so far as we must *choose* to resist the call of the trivial and to obey the call to worship. The example from the letter just cited shows that an encounter with God must be preceded by a sacrifice of time and energy.

The court of praise, then, is about sacrifice. To remind us of this there is a large bronze altar in the centre of this inner court. This altar was known as the altar of sacrifice and was the place where the priests would perform any one of five sacrifices: the sin offering, the trespass offering, the burnt offering, the meal offering and the peace offering. We shall look at these in more detail in the next chapter. For the time being, we need to focus on this altar and remember that praise is about giving, not receiving.

This truth needs to be emphasised in our day. So many people come to church to get a blessing rather than to be a blessing. Even more of us depend upon our feelings when it comes to the degree of our involvement in worship itself. As such we are largely a generation which has lost the vision for sacrificial praise. At worst we are a culture of consumers who shop around for the church which best suits us, and then who only opt into those parts of a worship event which make us feel good.

Yet we are often reminded in Scripture of a different kind of 'consumerism'. Jesus said, 'zeal for your house will *consume* me' (John 2:17). In other words, 'my passion for your Temple will be the death of me; it will cost me everything'. This is a very far cry from today's religious consumerism. Instead of selfishness, this statement shows us that true worship is not something which we consume, but rather something which consumes us. Jesus models a spirit of all-consuming self-denial. His words and actions remind us that 'We bring the sacrifice of praise into the house of the LORD' (Psalm 116:17).

One of the most powerful stories I have heard concerns a Christian who had an amazing singing voice. He learned that he had cancer of the tongue and that he was going to have to have drastic surgery. In hospital, as he prepared for his operation, he asked the surgeon whether he would be able to sing again. He was told that this would not be possible. The singer then sat himself up in bed and asked for a few moments to sing one last time, a song of praise to God:

> I'll praise my Maker while I've breath,
> And when my voice is lost in death,
> Praise shall employ my nobler power;
> My days of praise shall ne'er be past,
> While life, and thought, and being last,
> Or immortality endures.

Praise indeed is sacrifice.

As we begin our ministry of praise in the court of the priests, we can therefore do no better than to recall the exhortation, 'Through Jesus, therefore, let us continually offer up a sacrifice of praise – the fruit of lips that confess his name' (Hebrews 13:15). As we do this, we shall prepare in the most meaningful and appropriate way for the sacrifice which we must make in the next stage of prayer, as we put our sins to death through the power of the Cross.

Prayer

Dear Lord and Heavenly Father, help me now, through Jesus, to offer up a sacrifice of praise. I want to confess Jesus as Lord in the court of praise. I want to celebrate the supremacy of Jesus in a world that has reduced him to just a man. I want to praise Jesus for his uniqueness, his ultimacy and his deity.

Jesus, I praise you for the uniqueness of your name. I worship you because you are our Advocate in Heaven, the Bread of Life, the Consolation of Israel, the Door to Pastures New, Immanuel, God with us, the Friend of Sinners, our Great High Priest, the Holy One, Image of the Invisible God, Judge of All, King of Kings, Lord of Glory, Mighty God, the One and Only Son of Yahweh, the Prince of Peace and Righteous God, the Saviour of the World and our True Vine.

I praise you for your character and confess you, Jesus, as the Messiah, the Son of the Living God.

Lord Jesus, with countless other Kingdom priests, I praise you today in the inner court.

I bring a sacrifice of praise into the house of the Lord as I confess your name with my lips, and I stand in awe of you. Amen.

FOUR

The Altar of Sacrifice

Confession without change is just a game.
Tom Harris, *I'm OK. You're OK*

In the year 740 BC, Isaiah entered the court of the priests in the Temple in Jerusalem. He made his way into the holy place, and began his daily ministrations. Suddenly, the furniture and decor of the earthly Temple began to fade. In their place, new and heavenly counterparts started to emerge. In front of him, in what a few moments before had been the veiled entrance to the Holy of Holies, stood a great throne. On it, Isaiah saw Jehovah God, the Lord of all history and the Creator of the Universe. The long folds of his resplendent robes filled the sanctuary and flowed into the courts outside.

Above the throne, strange celestial beings hovered motionlessly. They were on both sides of the throne, calling out the antiphons of heaven in deep melodious voices. 'Holy', they cried on one side; 'Holy' they replied on the other. As their sonorous voices gained in strength, Isaiah became aware of the ground shaking beneath his feet: the stronger the voices of the angels, the stronger the tremor of the stone around him. The great portals of the sanctuary began to shudder. The porch began to sway. Great clouds of smoke appeared from nowhere and Isaiah was filled with indescribable terror.

The prophet sank to his knees and then fell prostrate on the cold and trembling floor. His eyes filled with tears and, out of the deepest recesses of his soul, came a loud and tremulous cry: 'Woe is me. I am ruined. For I am a man of unclean lips and I live among a people of unclean lips, and my eyes have seen the King, the Lord Almighty!'

A few seconds passed. Then, as suddenly as it had begun, the shaking finished. The Temple stood still. Out of the corner of his eye Isaiah saw one of the seraphs above the throne fly to a great bronze altar and delicately lift a glowing ember from a small fragrant censer. Then the seraph flew towards Isaiah. The sound of its six wings as it hovered overhead seemed deafening in the silence. Isaiah looked up tentatively, and as he did so the seraph touched the prophet's lips with the coal. A warm, cleansing fire went straight down his throat and passed quickly through the whole of his body, and as it did so, the seraph pronounced absolution: 'Your guilt is taken away and your sin atoned for.'

With that, Isaiah stood up in the sanctuary of God's house. He was forgiven, he was cleansed, and he was ready to hear God.

The Altar of Sacrifice

Entering the gates of thanksgiving, we are confronted by a brass altar, elevated above the level of the court by about 15 feet. We know that it was 30 feet long and was especially designed for various forms of sacrifice, but very little information is provided about this altar in Scripture. The writer of 2 Chronicles rather laconically remarks that 'Solomon made a bronze altar twenty cubits long, twenty cubits wide, and ten cubits high' (2 Chronicles 4:1). We do know that it was made of brass. Indeed, brass was the dominant metal in the court of the priests: the altar was brass, the great basin was brass, the small basins were made of brass, the two great pillars at the porch to the holy place were also brass. Since brass is symbolic of God's judgement in Scripture, we can see the significance of this. The court of the priests was decorated in brass because it was the place where sin was owned and dealt with.

In the Temple precincts the altar was the place of sacrifice. It was very likely the place from which the angels took the coals of fire in Isaiah chapter 6. Five different sacrifices ordained by God and given to Moses were conducted at this bronze altar in the court of the priests: first, the burnt offering (Leviticus 1); secondly, the grain offering (Leviticus 2); thirdly, the peace offering (Leviticus 3); fourthly, the sin offering (Leviticus 4) and finally, the guilt offering (Leviticus 5). Specific regulations are recorded in the Bible for each of these sacrifices.

The burnt offering was made every morning and evening by the priests on behalf of the whole of Israel. The priest took a bull, or a sheep, or a bird – young, male and without defect – and slaughtered it. The blood was then taken from the dead animal and sprinkled against the altar. The animal's carcass was then stripped and burnt on the altar where it would produce 'an aroma pleasing to the LORD' (Leviticus 1:9).

The grain offering (the only bloodless offering) accompanied either the burnt, sin or peace offering. It consisted of grain or fine flour being burnt on the altar, along with olive oil, salt and incense. The Hebrew word for 'grain offering' can also be translated as 'gifts'. This highlights its purpose: the grain offering was a gift set aside for God which was to accompany one of three other offerings. It was a sign of the sinner's humble devotion.

The peace offering was made three times a year at the major Jewish festivals. The main purpose behind this sacrifice was obviously 'peace'. The Hebrew word for peace, *shalom*, is often used of a peaceful or 'whole' relationship with God, with others, and with creation. The sacrifice itself consisted of the slaughter of an animal without defect. This could be offered on behalf of any of the many thousands of people who attended the three major Jewish festivals in the year.

The sin offering was a very specific sacrifice. It was designed for those who had sinned unintentionally. If an anointed priest, or the whole of Israel, or a leader, or a member of the community of Israel committed sins in ignorance (i.e. not realising at the time that they were sinning), then a sin offering was to be made by the priest as soon as the sin became known. Again, this involved the slaughter of a young animal.

The final offering was the guilt offering. This was traditionally known as 'the trespass offering' and was very similar to the sin offering. It was made in instances where restitution was feasible. In modern terms, if I stole a car from someone else, got caught and repented, the guilt offering would be made because I could return the car to the rightful owner. I would also find that I would have to pay a 20 per cent indemnity.

More important than these sacrifices was the sacrifice occurring once each year on the Day of Atonement. This is described in Leviticus 16 and was performed by the high priest who took incense and blood from the brazen altar and went into the Holy of Holies (which only he was allowed to enter, and only during this solemn festival during what in Old Testament times were called 'the days of awe').

Once behind the veil, the high priest arranged the burning, fragrant incense in a place where the smoke would cover the ark. After that he took some of the blood and sprinkled it with his finger seven times over the front of the cover of the ark. Next he slaughtered a goat and took its blood behind the curtain, repeating the same procedure.

The high priest then came out of the sanctuary with blood from both the bull and the goat, and sprinkled it over the altar of sacrifice in the outer court. He took hold of a live goat, laid both hands upon the animal's head, and confessed over it the sins of the people of Israel. All their wickedness and rebellion was placed upon the head of the goat. The high priest then sent the goat out into the desert in the care of a man especially appointed for the task. The 'scapegoat' carried these sins to a solitary place, where the man released it.

Following that, the high priest bathed himself in the laver of water and put on his normal, priestly garments. He then went to the great brazen altar in the court of the priests to make a burnt offering for both himself and the Israelite nation. He also burnt the fat of the sin offering on this altar. Once this holy day was complete, then the people were released from their sins and clean in the sight of the Lord.

The New Covenant Altar

Before we turn to the practice of confession we need to remember that this ancient system of sacrifice has been rendered redundant by the atoning death of Jesus on the Cross. Jesus is the Lamb of God who takes away the sin of the world (John 1:29, 36). Since lambs were slaughtered as a sin offering at Passover, this means that Calvary is the one perfect and final atonement for human sin. No more animals need to be slaughtered. No more offerings need to be burnt. Jesus has bridged the gap between humanity and God. Jesus has assumed our sin in his body on the Cross. He is Christ, the Passover Lamb, who has been sacrificed for us (compare 1 Corinthians 5:7). Thus the writer of the Hebrews declares:

> When Christ came as high priest of the good things that are already here, he went through the greater and more perfect tabernacle that is not man-made, that is to say, not a part of this creation. He did not enter by means of the blood of goats and calves; but he entered the Most Holy Place once and for all by his own blood, having obtained eternal redemption. The blood of goats and bulls and the ashes of a heifer sprinkled on those who are ceremonially unclean sanctify them so that they are outwardly clean. How much more, then, will the blood

of Christ, who through the eternal Spirit offered himself unblemished to God, cleanse our consciences from acts that lead to death, so that we may serve the Living God!

Hebrews 9:11–14

In our ministry of sacrifice we therefore come to a new altar. The old altar has been supplemented: there is now a Cross in the court of praise. On this new altar of sacrifice we will find no other blood than that shed by Jesus, which cleanses us from all unrighteousness (Hebrews 13:10). This is the altar where we now must bow with humility.

There are four things which we need to understand about God's new covenant altar of sacrifice as we approach the Cross for repentance. First of all, we need to see it as a place of sincerity – a place where we resolve to deal with the sin in our lives in an honest way. As John wrote, 'If we say we have no sin we deceive ourselves' (1 John 1:8). So the first step is to resolve to be ruthlessly real in owning and naming our sins. Secondly, we need to see the altar as a place of scrutiny, a place where we choose to examine our lives in the light of God's Word, in particular in the light of the Ten Commandments. Thirdly, we need to see this altar as a place of sacrifice – a place where we put sin to death. Fourthly, we must see it as a place of sanctification – a place where we are cleansed first of all through the blood of Christ, and secondly through the pure waters of the Holy Spirit.

A Place of Sincerity

The first thing to remember is that the new altar of sacrifice is a place of sincerity. At this point I find it helpful to meditate on a comment made by Tom Harris in his book *I'm OK. You're OK*. He wrote: 'Confession without change is just a game.' In other words, mere apology is not enough. Saying sorry without the intention to stop sinning makes a mockery of confession. True confession always involves change: a change of mind, a change of heart, and a change of behaviour.

Say, for example, that I am presently struggling with the problem of bad language. If I am really serious about repenting, then I will be looking for three levels of transformation.

First of all, I will be looking for a change of mind. Having tolerated this habit, I now look upon it as a serious sin. I *name* this habit for what it is. I see from God's Word (e.g. Colossians 3:8) that such language is offensive to a holy God. I understand that it is contrary to God's Word and destructive to my relationships and to my Christian witness.

Secondly, I will be looking for a change of heart. Having become convinced that my behaviour is sinful, I now become convicted of having sinned. I get in touch with my feelings about using bad language. I feel guilty. I am sad that I have grieved the Holy Spirit. I may even weep at the realisation of my sin. Like Isaiah, I begin to recognise that I am literally a man of unclean lips, living among a people of unclean lips. In the process, I begin to feel differently. I no longer *want* to sin in this way. I experience a change of heart.

Thirdly, I will be looking for a change of behaviour. I now co-operate with the Holy Spirit on a daily basis in what James calls 'the taming of the tongue' (James 3:1–12). I seek to work with the Lord in taking all my thoughts and words captive to the obedience of Jesus Christ. If I am very wise I might well ask another Christian to observe my behaviour and to watch out for compromise. Now, at last, repentance is bearing observable fruit. I am experiencing a change of behaviour.

The altar of sacrifice is therefore a place of total sincerity. Nothing less than complete honesty will do in the presence of the Lord.

A Place of Scrutiny

The second thing to note about this altar is that it is a place of scrutiny. Here we need to remember the words of Lamentations 3:40: 'Let us examine our ways and test them, and let us return to the Lord.' How, then, do we examine or scrutinise our lives?

If we look again at the altar of sacrifice in the Temple, we will notice that its measurements were all numerals of ten. The altar was ten cubits high, twenty cubits long, ten cubits wide. Why is this significant? As so often, the answer has to do with Jewish number symbolism. The number ten is the number of the Torah or the Law in the Old Testament. When Moses received the revelation of God's Law on Mount Sinai he received it in the form of the ten commandments. The numerals of ten in the altar of sacrifice point to the requirement to obey God's commandments. If we want to enter the holy place of God's presence, we need to scrutinise our lives and make sure that we have not broken any of the ten commandments. As John wrote, 'Everyone who sins breaks the Law; in fact, sin is lawlessness' (1 John 3:4).

The ten commandments are known as the Decalogue, after the Greek words *deca* (meaning ten) and *logos* (meaning command). They are summarised in Exodus 20 and Deuteronomy 5:

1. No other gods
2. No idolatry
3. No blasphemy
4. No abuse of the Sabbath
5. No disrespect for parents
6. No murder
7. No adultery
8. No stealing
9. No false testimony
10. No covetousness.

It is fair to say that the societies of Western Europe now virtually ignore the ten commandments. Countries in the West were, for hundreds of years, constructed around the Law of Moses. Their legal systems were based on it. Their stability depended upon it. However, the Age of Enlightenment produced a widespread secularism in which God was increasingly pushed to the sidelines. As a result, societies became increasingly post-Christian and, in the process, the commandments given to Moses became an ancient and dusty irrelevance.

In Great Britain, all ten commandments are openly flouted today. As British culture and society become increasingly alienated from God, people turn to idols such as money, status, success and sex as surrogate objects of worship or 'gods'. Everywhere, the names of God and of Jesus are taken in vain. There is no respect for Sunday as a holy day; it is now a day of trading like any other. The family unit is decaying rapidly; young people rebel against their parents – if they have parents. Murder is rife, even of babies, toddlers and the elderly. The sanctity of marriage has been forgotten; divorce costs Britain £4 million a day and adultery is on the increase. Stealing is widespread – from the secreting of unaccounted stationery to the taking and wrecking of other people's cars. With the breakdown of community, neighbours now fight and litigate over parking spaces and garden fences. Finally, in a culture designated as the 'me' generation, many regard the property of others as fair game.

Infringements of all the commandments are widespread today but one which is broken most flagrantly is the second, the prohibition against idolatry:

> You shall not make for yourself an idol in the form of anything in heaven above or in the waters below. You shall not bow down to them or worship them; for I, the Lord your God, am a jealous God, punishing the children for the sin of the fathers to the third and fourth generation of those who hate me, but showing love to a thousand of those who love me and keep my commandments.
>
> Deuteronomy 5:8–10

In Moses' day, idolatry was easy to spot. If a group of Israelites melted a precious metal, formed it into a large animal, then started bowing down to it and worshipping it, you could be fairly sure that they were suffering from a severe case of idolatry. It would not take the mind of a great saint to diagnose this condition. Idolatry was a *visible* phenomenon. Today, however, idolatry is more difficult to define because it is more invisible. We do not see people prostrate before large metal sculptures in our high streets or backyards. What we *do* see is people emotionally dependent upon various objects, substances, goals and relationships. We see people who are suffering from an idolatry which consists not of an overt devotion to a man-made idol but rather of a disguised obsession of the heart. Anything which, to use Luke Johnson's words, 'rivets my attention, centres my activity, preoccupies my mind, and motivates my action', is my god or my idol. As Johnson concludes, 'That in virtue of which I act is god; that for which I will give up anything else is my god.'[1]

St Augustine once wrote, 'idolatry is worshipping anything that ought to be used, or using anything that ought to be worshipped'. What, then, are the attachments or idols which are most prevalent today? The fact is, there are so many that it would be impossible to provide an exhaustive list of them. People seem to be dependent upon a great variety of things. All around us we can see examples of idolatrous attachment to food, shopping, clothes, home-making, DIY, sport, fitness, money, status, home technology, sex, relationships, ideologies, alcohol, prescription drugs, illicit drugs, chocolate, and so on. I have written extensively about these addictions or idols in my book *O Brave New Church: Confronting the Addictive Culture*[2] (also published by Darton, Longman and Todd). Here I examine the many different things to which people today become excessively attached. However, there are three idols which seem to grip and destroy people more than any other. As Richard Foster has rightly shown, these are the idols of money, sex and power.[3]

In 1 John 2:15–17, the apostle commands us not to love the world. He identifies three idols which are particularly dangerous: the lust of the flesh; the lust of the eyes; the pride of life. The lust of the flesh can be defined as the unbridled drive to express one's passion – specifically sexual passion. The lust of the eyes can be defined as the unbridled drive to amass our possessions – specifically material possessions. The pride of life can be defined as the unbridled drive to establish our position in life – specifically a position of status and dominance over others. These three drives, once activated, force a person onto a slippery slope of destructive lifestyle which I am describing as 'idolatry'. They are drives which encourage the worship of money, sex and power.

The power of these drives means that we, as Christians, must learn to be ruthless with any sign of idolatry in our own lives. We have to confront our idols through a process of self-scrutiny. That is why the apostle John ends his first letter with the words: 'Dear children, keep yourselves from idols.' John is urging us constantly to watch our own lives and make sure that we are not starting to become preoccupied with someone or something other than God. God will bless us in our sexuality, in our material needs and in our position in life just so long as they are all under his Lordship.

A Place of Sacrifice

Honest scrutiny must be followed by ruthless sacrifice. Sacrifice is a vivid metaphor for the confession of sin. The altar of sacrifice was, after all, a place of execution. In the era of the old covenant, animals were brutally killed on this altar. In the era of the new covenant, Jesus was also brutally killed. He was forced to carry a heavy cross-beam to a rubbish dump outside Jerusalem, where long iron spikes were hammered through the median nerve in his wrists and feet. The altar of sacrifice is therefore not a safe, hygienic place, neither in the Old nor in the New Testament. This altar has a suggestion of brutality about it. It is a place of finality, not a place of frivolity.

When Paul talks about dealing with sin he uses the violent language of sacrifice and of execution. In Colossians 3:5 he writes, 'Put to death, therefore, whatever belongs to your earthly nature.' The vocabulary here is extremely important. Notice that Paul does not say, 'Apologise to God.' Paul says 'put sin to death'. The word translated 'put to death' is *nekrosate*, an imperative form of the verb *nekroo*. In the noun form the word is *nekrosis*, the word used by Paul in 2 Corinthians 4:10 where he writes, 'We always carry about in our body the putting to death (*nekrosis*) of Jesus.' Paul is therefore speaking in violent terms in Colossians 3:5. In relation to our personal holiness, Paul is saying 'Be ruthless with the things of the earthly nature. Put them to death!'

Most of us have few problems putting an occasional sin to death, one that is, as it were, 'out of character' and rare. Where problems arise is in the termination of habitual sins, of addictive patterns of sinful behaviour. How do we deal with this kind of sin with finality? I believe we have a great deal to learn from those who help addicts – Alcoholics Anonymous (AA) and related groups. These bodies have a programme for dealing with addiction. I have adapted these steps so as to make them relevant for Christians who want to confess some area of their lives where habitual sin or addictive habits have taken control:

Step 1. I admit that I am powerless over my addiction – that my life has become unmanageable.

Step 2. I confess that the Holy Spirit, God's power, can restore me to wholeness.

Step 3. I make a decision to turn my will and my life over to the care of the living God.

Step 4. I make a searching and fearless moral inventory of myself.

Step 5. I admit to God, to myself, and to another trusted Christian friend the exact nature of my sins.

Step 6. I make myself ready to let God remove all my defects.

Step 7. I humbly ask the Lord to remove my shortcomings. In the company of trusted friends I renounce idolatry and pray for deliverance.

Step 8. I make a list of all persons I have harmed, and I become willing to make amends to them all.

Step 9. I make direct amends to such people wherever possible, except when to do so would injure them or others.

Step 10. I continue to make a personal inventory and when I go wrong, I promptly admit it.

Step 11. I seek through prayer to improve my relationship with God, praying for more love and more power to live a holy and a healed life.

Step 12. Having had a spiritual awakening as the result of these steps, I try to carry this message to others.

There are a number of things we can learn about ruthless confession from this 12-step programme. First, we learn the value of community. Christians have a highly individualistic conception of repentance: we think that we can destroy our idols all on our own. AA and related groups know that freedom is only possible through community. Addicts need the help of others if they are to be liberated – and so do we (James 5:16).

Secondly, we have a lot to learn from the ninth step, in which the addict is encouraged to go and apologise to all those who have been harmed by his behaviour. This again is pertinent to confession. The AA programme reminds us of the old Christian truth that the circle of confession should be related to the circle of commission. If I have committed a sin against God, I confess to God. If I have committed a sin against someone else, I confess to them. If I have committed a sin against the Church, I confess to the Church, and so on.

Thirdly, we have a lot to learn from the realism of this programme. Addicts know that they will be tempted to fall again. They are therefore not complacent. They keep on subjecting their lives to a fearless moral inventory. This too is relevant. Although we make every effort to repent truly, we recognise our weakness as human beings and that we may be tempted in similar areas again. We therefore take steps to ensure that we do not knowingly enter contexts of temptation, areas of life where we will be vulnerable to falling again.

A Place of Sanctification

The altar is therefore a place of sacrifice and this of course means that we have a part to play in the matter of personal sanctification – the process by which we become more holy. We have to be sincere. We have to scrutinise our lives. We have to own, name and terminate our sins with the help of the Holy Spirit.

This needs emphasising in our day. Most people forget their own part in this process. People have one of two understandings of sanctification. These two views we might call a *feminine* and a *masculine* view. If some psychologists are right when they say that masculinity is about 'initiating' and femininity is about 'receiving', then the masculine view of sanctification is this: 'I become holy by striving to do what the Bible tells me to do.' The feminine view of sanctification says, 'It is not for me to take the initiative. Sanctification is a matter of me receiving more and more of God's Holy Spirit. All I need to do is to keep open. God will do the rest.'

Both of these perspectives are half true. There is a masculine aspect to sanctification. When Paul says, 'Put sin to death,' he is addressing Christians in the church at Colossae. They, not God, are the subject of the imperative, *nekrosate*. It is they who must work and strive towards holiness. Indeed we see this everywhere in Paul's writings. It is we who must take the initiative in the battle against the flesh. We are to be the executioners of sin. But there is undoubtedly a feminine aspect as well. Not only are we to fight, to wrestle, to struggle and to strive; we are also to remember that we are not alone in the battle. The Holy Spirit is at work within us to restore the image of Jesus Christ in our lives. That is why Paul encourages us to put to death the deeds of the body by the power of the Spirit (Romans 8:13). The command to terminate sin (*thanatoute*, 'mortify') is accompanied by the assurance that the Holy Spirit will assist us in this task. We are not alone!

So when Paul says, 'Put sin to death' he is showing that we have personal responsibility for dealing with sin. We are accountable to God in the area of holiness. This of course is a huge challenge. As John Flavel once said, 'It is easier to cry against one thousand sins of others than to kill one of your own.' But, at the same time, God does not leave us to wage the war against our flesh on our own. If we cooperate with his Holy Spirit then the war will be won a great deal more easily.

Sanctification is therefore vital. We need to clean out the temple of our bodies on a regular basis in prayer. Just as Jesus drove out the money-changers and the pigeon-fanciers in the Temple in Jerusalem, so Jesus drives out the sin and idolatry in our bodies. Just as Jesus cleansed the Temple in Jerusalem in the yesterday of history, so he cleanses the temple of my body in the today of my discipleship, and in the tomorrow of my walk with him. Jesus is the same yesterday, today and forever (Hebrews 13:8). What he did in the Temple nearly 2,000 years ago he will go on doing in the temples of our bodies and in the new temple of his Church.

As if to remind us of this promise of cleansing, there is not only an altar in the court of praise. There is also a molten sea – a huge bronze basin which rested on 12 bronze oxen (2 Chronicles 4:2–6, 15; 1 Kings 7:23–6, 44; 1 Chronicles 18:8). This contained water for the purification of the priests (2 Chronicles 4:6). If the brazen altar is a place of making sacrifice, the molten sea is a place of receiving cleansing; if the one is a place of blood, the other is a place of water. This should remind us of Calvary, for on the Cross there flowed both blood and water from the side of the Saviour (John 19:34). As the old revival hymn puts it:

On the Mount of Crucifixion
Fountains opened deep and wide;
Through the floodgates of God's mercy
Flowed a vast and gracious tide.
Grace and love, like mighty rivers,
Poured incessant from above,
And heaven's peace and perfect justice
Kissed a guilty world in love.

We should never forget that the pardon and purity which we receive at the altar of sacrifice are gifts of Calvary.

The Art of Confession

So the third stage of prayer in the Temple of God's presence requires that we should spend time before the new altar of sacrifice that is the Cross of Jesus Christ – a place of sincerity, of scrutiny, of sacrifice and of sanctification. Having looked backwards in thanksgiving (stage 1), and upwards in praise (stage 2), we now look inwards in confession (stage 3). Kneeling before the altar of sacrifice, we therefore need to cultivate the ability to look inwards in a healthy way. In doing this we must beware of two extremes: toxic self-denigration on the one hand, and blind self-righteousness on the other. Self-righteousness is a particular danger. That is why Jesus told this parable:

> Two men went up to the Temple to pray, one a Pharisee and the other a tax collector. The Pharisee stood up and prayed about himself: 'God, I thank you that I am not like other men – robbers, evildoers, adulterers – or even like this tax collector. I fast twice a week and give a tenth of all I get.' But the tax collector stood at a distance. He would not even look up to heaven, but beat his breast and said, 'God, have mercy on me, a sinner.'
>
> Luke 18:9–14

We must be careful not to indulge in Pharisaical fantasies about our level of righteousness. The Pharisee was guilty precisely of this. But at the same time we must also be careful not to be tempted into diseased self-hatred. Self-righteousness and self-hatred are both forms of self-indulgence. They are altogether too influenced by our own view of ourselves, rather than by God's view of us. The example of the publican shows that it is possible to grieve about our inner state without feeling rejected by God. Jesus said of this man that he, not the Pharisee, went home justified before God. In other words, he went home knowing that he had been, in the words of the hymn, 'ransomed, healed, restored, forgiven'.

So how can we make the most of our time at the Cross, confessing our sins? Here are some options:

Spontaneous confession
Sometimes the actual practice of confession involves a simple cry of the heart. Like the tax collector, we weep before God and cry, 'God, have mercy on me, a sinner.'

Scriptural confession
At other times, it might be more appropriate to engage in a meditation on the ten commandments. This might involve thinking carefully about each commandment, and then allowing the Holy

Spirit to illuminate areas of sin in ourselves and in our society. Something like this may sometimes be more fitting:

1. *You shall have no other gods but me.* Lord, I acknowledge you as the One True Living God, revealed in Jesus of Nazareth. Keep me pure in my devotion to you. Help me not to be deceived by the voices around me into thinking that there are other gods beside you. Help me to make a firm stand in this pluralistic culture and to say, 'There is one God, the God and Father of our Lord Jesus Christ.' Help me to love you with all of my heart, all of my soul, all of my mind, and all of my strength today and every day.

2. *You shall not make for yourself any idol.* Lord, help me not to be over-dependent upon anyone or anything other than you. You are an all-sufficient God. I do not need money, sex or power to be a fulfilled person. Today I renounce money, sex, power and all their works in my life. I ask you to help me to be obedient to the ethical requirements of the Kingdom. Help me to live a lifestyle of detachment, not attachment. Help me to be addicted to Jesus alone.

3. *You shall not dishonour the name of the Lord your God.* Lord, keep me from ever taking your name – or the name of your Son – in vain. Today I renounce blasphemy and all foul language. I take every thought and word of mine captive to the obedience of Jesus Christ and I ask that you would give me clean lips in this generation of unclean lips. I put this sin to death on the altar.

4. *Remember the Lord's Day and keep it holy.* Forgive me that Sunday is not always the highlight of my week. Forgive me that so often I endure it and spoil it. Help me to rejoice and be glad in this day that you have made. Help me to set it apart from all other days. Lord, make Sunday a truly Christ-centred day.

5. *Honour your father and your mother.* Lord, I think of where I am today in my relationship with my parents. Help me to honour, revere and obey my parents – even in the trivial tasks of telephoning or letter-writing. And Lord, forgive our nation for breaking this commandment on such a massive scale. Heal families. Restore biblical values in the home.

6. *You shall not murder.* Have mercy upon me, Lord. I

remember that Jesus said that to have a violent thought about someone was to commit murder in your eyes. Forgive me for the aggressive fantasies I have had about those who have hurt me. Help me to forgive and to be reconciled, not to harbour resentment and bitterness towards others.

7. *You shall not commit adultery.* Lord, I remember today that you created marriage and that you invented sex. I therefore submit to your Word in these matters. Help me to remember your abhorrence of *poneia* – of sexual intercourse outside of marriage. I reflect again on your call to sexual holiness in 1 Thessalonians 4:3–8 and say, 'Lord, forgive me for all traces of sexual immorality.' I conduct a fearless moral inventory of my sexuality right now and I put to death on the altar all those thoughts, words and actions which are contrary to your Word. I ask you to forgive me.

8. *You shall not steal.* Lord, help me not to be worldly in this area. Forgive me that I so often lack complete integrity in the matter of stationery, expenses, bills and taxes. Help me to see even misdemeanours as infringements of this eighth commandment. Help me to see them as serious sin. Please forgive me for my worldliness. Help me to be different by putting to death all compromise in this area.

9. *You shall not be a false witness.* Lord, I ask you to forgive me for the things that I have said against others – cynical, destructive, evil things. Help me to live in love and peace with all people. Help me not to slander and criticise in order to be popular or accepted. Forgive me that my relationships with those who are my neighbours are not all that they could be. Lord have mercy upon me. I put to death the habit of false testimony. I choose instead to speak the truth in love.

10. *You shall not covet.* Lord, I admit that I sometimes look at someone else's house, someone else's salary, someone else's lifestyle, someone else's spouse, and I wish that I had what they had. I put the sin of covetousness to death and I choose to celebrate with a dance of gratitude that which you have, so graciously, given to me.

Structured confession

Also helpful is the use of set prayers of confession, especially when there is no obvious sense of sin in our lives. I often use an adapted

and personalised version of the prayer of confession in the
Anglican liturgy:

> Almighty God, my Heavenly Father,
> I confess that I have sinned against you
> and against others,
> in thought, word and deed,
> through negligence, through weakness,
> through my own deliberate fault.
> For the sake of your Son Jesus Christ,
> who died for me,
> please forgive me for all that is past,
> and grant that I may serve you
> in newness of life,
> to the glory of your holy name,
> Amen.

It can also be helpful to use the following prayer of confession,
known as the *widduy*, which forms the heart of Yom Kippur. The
section I am about to cite is called the *al het* and is again an
adapted, personalised version:[4]

> May it be your will, O Lord our God and God of our fathers,
> to forgive me for all my sins, to pardon me for all my
> iniquities, and to grant me remission for my transgressions.
> For the sin which I have committed before you under
> compulsion, or of my own will . . .
> For the sin which I have committed before you through the
> hardening of my heart . . .
> For the sin which I have committed before you out of
> ignorance . . .
> For the sin which I have committed before you through the
> utterances of my lips . . .
> For the sin which I have committed before you by
> unchastity . . .
> For the sin which I have committed before you openly and
> secretly . . .
> For all these, O God of forgiveness, forgive me, pardon me,
> grant me remission . . .
> Through Jesus Christ, who died for me. Amen.

Whichever form of confessional prayer one uses, the important thing is to come to the brazen altar prepared for sincerity, scrutiny, sacrifice and sanctification.

Above all, it is important to come to the altar with trust in God. God promises in his Word: 'I will forgive their wickedness and will remember their sins no more' (Jeremiah 31:34).

Here we are embraced with the amazing grace of God. God says, 'I will completely forget the sins which you confess.' This means that when I truly repent of sin in my life, from that moment on God suffers from a permanent and complete forgetfulness concerning that sin! I call this forgetfulness 'divine amnesia'. Divine amnesia comes into operation when we pray to God, saying, 'I've done it again, Lord.' If we truly repented the first time, God will reply, 'Done what again?'

So, come to the altar trusting in God's promises. God is omnipotent, yes. But there is one thing he will not and cannot do, and that is lie. So if God promises it, that should settle it. He will keep his word. He will remember our sins no more.

Prayer

Merciful Father, I confess all my sins before you now. I particularly want to repent of the following . . .

I put them all to death on the Cross through the power of the Spirit. In the mighty name of Jesus Christ I terminate all these things that grieve your Holy Spirit. I ask you to help me to change, not just in my thoughts and in my feelings, but also in my behaviour.

Lord, pardon me through the blood of Christ and cleanse me in the water of your Spirit. Please apply all the benefits of the finished work of the Cross to my life. Please remove all my sins as far from me as the east is from the west and please, in accordance with your promise, remember them no more. Make it 'just-as-if-I'd' never sinned.

Thank you, Jesus, for the blood and the water in the court of praise. Thank you for the Cross.

Help me to know that I am now 'ransomed, healed, restored, forgiven'.

Amen.

The Holy Place

O Thou, who camest from above
The pure celestial fire to impart,
Kindle a flame of sacred love
On the mean altar of my heart.

Charles Wesley

Further Up and Further In

We have now passed through God's gates with thanksgiving in our hearts, entered the inner court with praise on our lips, and confessed our sins at the new altar of sacrifice, the Cross. Having received God's pardon and cleansing, we now climb the steps to the sanctuary, a great building known as the Holy Place. Before us are two bronze pillars which stand before the huge portals to the sanctuary. This is the last time we shall see anything made of bronze as we pray in the Temple of the Lord's presence. Everything from now on will be made of gold rather than bronze. The bronze of judgement is now replaced by the gold of majesty. Every item of furniture in the Holy Place will be radiant and brilliant with gold.

All this shows how our ministry as Kingdom priests is, in reality, a journey into the Father's presence. The title of this book is *Drawing Near to God*. That is because I see the different stages of prayer as a gradual pilgrimage in which we go 'further up and further in' to the heart of God. The change from bronze to gold signifies the progress of this journey. The need to climb up to the sanctuary has the same effect. All the time we are obeying the call in James 4:8: 'Come near to God and he will come near to you.'

And so, as you continue this journey, I invite you to imagine the Lord Jesus Christ, the Great High Priest of the New Covenant, leading you through the doorway of the sanctuary, into the hall, and then onwards to various parts of the Holy Place and its furniture. Imagine him walking among the lampstands, guiding you through the ministries associated with the Holy Place, and helping you to pray according to his will and in his name.

The Table of Shewbread

The first place where we pause to pray in the Holy Place is at the golden table of shewbread. This table was carefully tended by the priests. Thus we read in 1 Chronicles that:

The duty of the Levites was to help Aaron's descendants in the service of the Temple of the LORD: to be in charge of the courtyards, the side rooms, the purification of all sacred things and the performance of other duties at the house of God. They were in charge of the bread set out on the table, the flour for the grain offerings, the unleavened wafers, the baking and the mixing, and all measurements of quantity and size.

1 Chronicles 23:28–9

This table was made of wood but was overlaid with gold. It was two feet high, three feet long and about 18 inches wide. On the top of the table were 12 pieces of unleavened shewbread. These were in two piles of six pieces. Every week, on the Sabbath, the priests replenished the shewbread. The old bread was theirs to eat. The new bread was to remain in the Holy Place until the following Sabbath.

The symbolism of the shewbread is this: the 12 pieces of bread represent the 12 tribes of Israel; the bread itself represents God's gracious provision of bread from heaven ('manna') when the Israelites were hungry in the desert. The golden table of shewbread therefore reminds us of the importance of petitionary prayer, of praying for our own, personal needs. It reminds us of the petition in the disciple's prayer, 'Give us this day our daily bread'.

So our first duty in the holy place is to petition for our own needs. Jesus himself encouraged us to petition when he said, 'Ask, and it will be given to you; seek, and you will find; knock, and the door will be opened to you' (Matthew 7:7). Jesus was legitimating the practice of self-orientated prayer. He was actually encouraging us to spend time praying for ourselves. He was telling us to

A – ask
S – seek
K – knock

We are permitted to pray for our own needs.

Praying for Our Daily Bread

Many people have real difficulties with this kind of prayer. Most of these problems stem from a genuine sense of triviality; in other words, from the feeling that our needs are too small for God's attention. Consequently, many people never pray for the Father's help with the supposedly little things. They decide not to pray because they honestly feel that their need is too small and that God's time is too limited.

But God the Father is not a dad who has little time for the trivial. He is a Father who has the same amount of time for everyone and for everything. That is because in heaven there is no time. The Father is addressing our needs from a point beyond time and space. He can therefore be meeting my need in the UK at the same time as he is meeting the needs of others in Africa! God is not confined as we are. We can therefore approach him with confidence.

Notice that it is our most basic needs that God is interested in hearing about. That is why it is so important that we see the significance of the word 'bread' in the petition, 'Give us this day our daily *bread*'. There could hardly be anything more mundane than bread – there are few things which we take more for granted! Yet it is daily bread that Jesus says we should pray for. Not so much luxury holidays, or huge salaries, or expensive meals, but *bread*.

There is therefore plenty of justification for coming to the golden table and for asking the Lord to meet our needs. This is not a place where we demand luxuries. It is a place where we ask for 'the bare necessities of life'. That is why Jesus says in Matthew 7:9–11:

> Which of you, if his son asks for bread, will give him a stone? Or if he asks for a fish, will give him a snake? If you, then, though you are evil, know how to give good gifts to your children, how much more will your Father in heaven give good gifts to those who ask him!

The Father longs to hear us asking for good gifts; that is, gifts that are good in the sight of God, and good for us. God longs to give us those things which will help us to live in harmony with his will.

This last point is extremely important: God longs to give us those things which will enable us to fulfil our God-given purpose. In other words, he promises those things which are consistent both with his character and with his plan. He does not promise us things that are not consonant with his character.

This truth requires emphasis in our times. Today there is a growing body of Christians all over the world who are employing some of the values of 'prosperity Christianity' in the practice of petition. Many are taking the words of Jesus in John 14:14 at face value: 'You may ask me for *anything* in my name and I will give it to you.' These words are used by prosperity teachers to suggest that we have guaranteed access to the 'blessings' of health and wealth. All we have to do is 'name it and claim it'. Did not Jesus say 'ask me for *anything*'? 'Well then,' say the prosperity teachers, 'ask for whatever you want and just believe for it!'

This kind of teaching is dangerous. The problem with it is that it does not take into consideration what Jesus meant by 'asking in his name'. In the Jewish culture of Jesus' day, a person's name summed up their whole personality. Their name was symbolic of their character. When Jesus said, 'You may ask me for anything in my name', he was therefore saying, 'You may ask me for the kinds of things which I myself would ask for.' Since it is inconceivable to think of Jesus ever asking for financial prosperity for his own sake, there can be no grounds for self-indulgence in petitionary prayer. Indeed, we should heed the warning given by James, the brother of the Lord Jesus: 'When you ask, you do not receive, because you ask with wrong motives, that you may spend what you get on your pleasures' (James 4:3). This sober statement alerts us to the need to come before the Father with honest motives.

The Practice of Petition

At the same time, we know that the Father desires to give good gifts to those who ask. Good gifts, in my view, are those gifts which enable us to function more effectively as disciples of the Lord Jesus. In this area we can have confidence. As the apostle John wrote:

> This is the confidence we have in approaching God: that if we ask anything according to his will, he hears us. And if we know that he hears us – whatever we ask – we know that we have what we asked of him.
>
> 1 John 5:14–15

So if physical pain or illness is preventing us from working for the Kingdom, it is not wrong to go to the Father and ask for relief from distress, for healing from illness. What father would refuse to comfort his child if that child was in pain, or needed a bandage? So it is with our Heavenly Father. We can come to him asking for healing from our hurts and illnesses.

The same goes not only for physical but also for material needs. If lack of money is causing us to focus more on essential needs than the business of the Kingdom, we should ask the Father for help in meeting our needs. I can remember many an occasion when I had to go to my father when I got into trouble financially at university. He was always willing to set me back on my feet again, though he was not always able to! How much more will our Heavenly Father be concerned that we should not worry about our lives, about what we will eat or drink or wear (Matthew 6:25–34)? How proper it is, therefore, to take our essential material needs to God in prayer, and then to trust him as *Jehovah Jireh* to provide what is right for us.

The same goes for other needs, in particular those relating to our emotions. If anxiety or depression is weighing us down and debilitating us in our work for the Lord, then it is here – at the golden table of shewbread – that we should cast our anxiety upon the Lord, knowing that he cares for us (1 Peter 5:7). It is here that we should plead with him for comfort, help, clarity, direction, wholeness. Whatever the nature of our dark night, God will want to walk there with us and guide us to the dawn of a new day.

The Golden Lampstands

If the Father is concerned about our physical, material and emotional needs, he is also concerned about all our other needs. He is particularly concerned to meet our spiritual needs. Here I find the golden lampstands a useful symbol and memory aid. The golden lampstands remind me of the spiritual resources which God graciously provides for his children.

One of the duties of the priests in the Temple was to rekindle the lampstands or *menorhot* (*menorah*, singular). There were ten of these in the Holy Place, five on each side of the chamber (1 Kings 7:49). Each of these was fashioned according to the instructions in Exodus 25:31–40:

> Make a lampstand of pure gold and hammer it out, base and shaft; its flower-like cups, buds and blossoms shall be of one piece with it. Six branches are to extend from the sides of the lampstand – three on one side and three on the other . . . The buds and branches shall all be of one piece with the golden lampstand, hammered out of pure gold. Then make it seven lamps and set them up on it so that they light the space in front of it. Its wick trimmers and trays are to be of pure gold. A talent of pure gold is to be used for the lampstand and all these accessories. See that you make them according to the pattern shown you on the mountain.

From the time of the early Church, the *menorah* has been seen as a symbol of the so-called sevenfold gifts of the Spirit.[1] The basis for this is the prophecy concerning the Messiah in Isaiah 11:2–3a:

> The Spirit of Yahweh will rest on him –
> the spirit of wisdom and of understanding,
> the spirit of counsel and of might,
> the spirit of the knowledge and fear of Yahweh,
> and he will delight in the fear of Yahweh.

The central branch of the *menorah* was understood to symbolise the Holy Spirit. The other three pairs of branches were understood to symbolise different manifestations or gifts of the Holy Spirit. The first pair, wisdom and understanding, were seen as

manifestations relating to the mind or the intellect. The second pair, counsel and might, were seen to relate to planning and strength. The third pair, the knowledge and the fear of Yahweh, were seen as gifts to help us in our relationship with the Father. This symbolism lies behind the words of the ancient hymn which begins:

> Come, Holy Ghost, our souls inspire,
> And lighten with celestial fire.
> Thou the anointing Spirit art,
> Who dost Thy sevenfold gifts impart.

This hymn is itself a good example of petitionary prayer, of asking for the good gifts of the Holy Spirit. Notice that the hymn speaks of the 'sevenfold gifts', corresponding to the seven branches of the *menorah*.

Petitioning for Spiritual Needs

So we are reminded by the golden *menorah* of the importance of asking for spiritual, not just physical, resources. Luke's version of Jesus' promise cited earlier makes this very plain: 'If you, then, though you are evil, know how to give good gifts to your children, how much more will your Father in heaven give the Holy Spirit to those who ask him!' Where Matthew's version reads, 'how much more will your Father in heaven give good gifts', Luke's version reads, 'how much more will your Father in heaven give the Holy Spirit'.

There are many spiritual gifts which we can ask for.[2] The following is a list of just some of them, and they are greater in number than just seven.

1. *Prophecy* (Romans 12:6; 1 Corinthians 12:10), an anointing in which a person is enabled to communicate God's will to a church through a vision, dream, picture, scripture, message or impression. It often involves a predictive dimension.

2. *Teaching* (Romans 12:7; Ephesians 4:11; 1 Corinthians 12:28), an anointing in which a person is enabled to expound and apply the Word of God in such a way that the listener is impacted by a sense of revelation, and then personal transformation.

3. *Encouragement* (Romans 12:8), an anointing in which a person is led to say or write something which builds up a fellow Christian in the faith.

4. *Evangelism* (Ephesians 4:11). While all are called to share the Gospel, some are given a special endowment or ability in this work. This is the gift of evangelism: an anointing in which a person is given the power to know with whom the Gospel should be shared, when it should be shared, and how.

5. *Hospitality* (1 Peter 4:9), an anointing in which a person is enabled to open his or her home to others. It is also an anointing in which Christians are enabled to invite and welcome outsiders into a church fellowship.

6. *Apostleship* (1 Corinthians 12:28; Ephesians 4:11), an anointing in which God empowers a person to go out from a church-base to establish a new church somewhere else.

7. *Leadership* (Romans 12:8; 1 Thessalonians 5:12), an anointing in which a person is given the ability to lead people in such a way that they want to follow.

8. *Mercy* (Romans 12:8), an anointing in which a person is moved by divine compassion to acquire and to give aid to the poor, the suffering and the oppressed.

9. *Pastoral care* (Ephesians 4:11), an anointing in which God

gives a person a heart to shepherd or look after a body of believers with great sensitivity and with practical care.

10. *Administration* (1 Corinthians 12:28), an anointing in which a person is enabled to draw up and maintain rotas, to make plans, to keep accounts, and the like.

11. *Craftsmanship* (Exodus 31:3–6), an anointing in which a person is enabled to use artistic gifts for the Church (e.g. composing songs, playing musical instruments, creating banners, drawing pictures, writing poetry).

12. *Giving* (Romans 12:9), an anointing in which someone is especially motivated to give of self, time and/or money for the work of the Church.

13. *Helping* (1 Corinthians 12:28), an anointing in which someone is especially enabled to give practical help, such as setting up rooms, clearing up chairs.

14. *Knowledge* (1 Corinthians 12:8), an anointing in which a person is given a supernatural insight into the ways of God. This is given directly by the Holy Spirit, not learned by natural means.

15. *Wisdom* (1 Corinthians 12:8), an anointing in which a person is empowered to say just the right thing, to just the right person, at just the right time.

16. *Faith* (1 Corinthians 12:9; 13:2), an anointing in which a person is given special confidence and conviction that God will achieve what seems, from a human point of view, to be impossible.

17. *Miracles* (1 Corinthians 12:10), an anointing in which a person is empowered by the Spirit to be a channel through which the seemingly impossible is achieved.

18. *Tongues* (1 Corinthians 12:10), an anointing in which a person is given a new language by the Holy Spirit, either for personal or for public use.

19. *Interpretation* (1 Corinthians 12:10, 30), an anointing in which a person is enabled to translate a public message uttered in tongues.

20. *Healing* (1 Corinthians 12:9, 30), an anointing in which a person is empowered by God to minister healing to those suffering from physical, emotional or spiritual affliction.

21. *Discernment* (1 Corinthians 12:10), an anointing in which a person is equipped to know when someone's words or actions

are motivated by the Holy Spirit, their human spirit or by unholy spirits.

As I minister to the Lord in the Holy Place, the golden lampstands remind me that it is good to petition for these gifts as the need arises. In other words, it is right to ask for certain gifts for myself when it is obvious that I cannot minister effectively without them.

The Golden Altar of Incense

A large part of our ministry in the sanctuary is thus taken up with petitionary prayer. At the same time, we must recognise that the main focus of the Holy Place was not the table of shewbread. Nor was it the ten golden lampstands. It was the golden altar of incense at the very end of the sanctuary. This was one of two altars in the Temple. The first was the bronze altar of sacrifice in the heart of the court of the priests. The second was a place of intercession and was made of gold. It was situated right in front of the veil which separated the Holy Place from the Holy of Holies. The instructions for the making of this altar were given by the Lord to Moses:

> Make an altar of acacia wood for burning incense. It is to be square, a cubit long and a cubit wide, and two cubits high – its horns of one piece with it. Overlay the top and all the sides and the horns with pure gold, and make a gold moulding around it . . . Put the altar in front of the curtain that is before the Ark of the Testimony – before the atonement cover that is over the Testimony – where I will meet with you. Aaron must burn fragrant incense on the altar every morning when he tends the lamps. He must burn incense again when he lights the lamps at twilight so that incense will burn regularly before the LORD for generations to come.
>
> Exodus 30:1–6

The Prayers of the Saints

The incense has a specific symbolism. In both the Old and the New Testament, the incense which rose to the heavens through the

roof of the Temple represented the prayers of the saints (living and departed), offered both in the morning and the evening. Thus, in Psalm 141:2, David cries:

> May my prayer be set before you
> like incense;
> May the lifting up of my hands
> be like the evening sacrifice.

In the New Testament, we are actually given a vision of the prayers of God's people as they ascend like incense to God's throne:

> Another angel, who had a golden censer, came and stood at the altar. He was given much incense to offer, with the prayers of all the saints, on the golden altar before the throne. The smoke of the incense, together with the prayers of the saints, went up before God from the angel's hand. Then the angel took the censer, filled it with fire from the altar, and hurled it on the earth; and there came peals of thunder, rumblings, flashes of lightning and an earthquake.
>
> Revelation 8:3–5

For me the incense on the altar of the sanctuary represents intercession. Intercessory prayer is to be distinguished from petitionary prayer. Petitionary prayer is praying for my personal needs. Intercessory prayer is praying for the needs of others. It is standing in the gap on someone else's behalf. So while the shewbread and the lampstands remind me of God's call to prayer for myself, the golden altar of incense reminds me of God's call to prayer for other people. As Charles Brent once said, 'intercessory prayer might be defined as loving our neighbour on our knees'.

Intercessory prayer is accordingly one of the highest forms of love. When we pray from the heart for someone, we are showing that we truly love them. In this regard it is important for us to remember that the table where the incense burns is an altar. Altars speak of sacrifice. Love speaks of sacrifice. When we undertake intercessory prayer, when we stand in the gap on behalf of another, it costs us. It costs in terms of time, in terms of energy, in terms of love. As J. H. Jowett wrote, 'All vital praying makes a drain on a person's vitality. True intercession is a sacrifice, a bleeding sacrifice.'

The Importance of Intercession

Why is intercessory prayer so important? Paul gives us the answer in Romans 8. In verses 18–39, he provides a magnificent description of the relationship between the creation and the Creator. The cosmos is not the same as God, as in pantheism. But the cosmos is not unrelated to God, as in deism. Rather, the Holy Spirit is at work within the cosmos, and the Holy Spirit is the immanent presence of the transcendent Creator. This means that the cosmos is inhabited by God's presence, but that God is still simultaneously beyond it. He is both in the world and outside it at the same time. The go-between, as it were, is the Holy Spirit.

Paul's charismatic or Spirit-oriented understanding of the relationship between creation and Creator is a subtle one. He knows that the world was subjected to destruction through the Fall, but he also knows that the coming of Jesus has brought a new power into the universe. This power is not some nebulous energy but rather the presence of the Kingdom of God, inaugurated on earth in the ministry of the historical Jesus. Since the coming of Jesus, the Holy Spirit has been at work restoring the fallen and decaying fabric of the cosmos. He has been intimately and passionately involved in every part of the created order, repairing the ubiquitous damage of the Fall, and helping the world on its new journey towards that end-point when the Kingdom of God will be fully established here on earth.

In the meantime we live between the arrival of the Kingdom (the first coming of Jesus) and its final consummation (the second coming of Jesus). In this 'eschatological tension', as the theologians call it, there is still much suffering in the world. The creation has not yet been fully liberated from its bondage to decay nor from its deep groaning caused by man's first disobedience. There are still floods, famines, earthquakes and diseases.

It is for this reason that the ministry of intercession is so important. To be sure, intercessory prayer will disappear when the Lord Jesus Christ returns. What need of intercession will there be when there are no more disasters, no more hospitals, no more funerals and no more tears? But that day is in the future. So in the meantime, there is a great need for intercessory prayer. God has given us the task of intercessory prayer as one of the instruments by which his Kingdom advances on the earth. Until God's perfect future is an eternal present, intercessory prayer will consequently be essential. Something world-changing and history-making is taking place every time we stand at the altar of incense and pray in the Spirit.

The Heights of Intercession

While we may see the importance of intercessory prayer, many of us often struggle to know what actually to pray. Here again, Romans 8 comes to the rescue. In verses 26–27, Paul rightly says that we do not know what we ought to pray for. We are, in short, stuck. We see the need to pray; we may even see the needs which need praying for. But the actual performance of intercession brings us up short. We are straight away confronted by a sense of inadequacy. What do we actually say? It is at this point that Paul brings us some words of encouragement. He assures us that the same Holy Spirit who is at work within the created order comes to our aid. The Spirit helps us in our weakness. He himself intercedes for us 'with groans that words cannot express'. He himself intercedes for the saints *in us*, and in accordance with God's will.

What is going on when the Spirit helps us in this way? Put simply, the Holy Spirit, at the moment of our speechlessness, gathers us up and joins our minds with that of the Ascended Lord Jesus. Jesus, we read in Romans 8:34, is he who died, who was raised to life, and who is now at the right hand of God *interceding for us*. So when we enter into intercessory prayer, the Holy Spirit lifts us up into the presence of the Ascended Christ, and joins our prayers with his before the Father. The Holy Spirit incorporates us in that constant stream of prayer which is going on in heaven – prayer which is ministered by the Son to the Father. This means that, in our priestly ministry of intercession, the Holy Spirit joins us with the ministry of our Great High Priest. He helps us to know the mind of Christ, who is the 'Intercessor, Friend of Sinners' (1 Corinthians 2:6–16), the one who identified with sinners by being numbered among the transgressors (Isaiah 53:12).

For this reason we must invite the Holy Spirit to lift us up and join our prayers with those of the Ascended Lord. The good news is that Paul assures us that the Holy Spirit is available to us in our intercessory ministry. Before beginning to intercede, I therefore like to invite the fire of God's Spirit to descend upon the censer of my heart and ignite the raw material of my prayer into a fragrant offering. Just occasionally I have actually detected the smell of incense when speaking about this kind of prayer, or engaging in it. Not long ago I preached a message about 'Restoring the Altar of Incense in Our Lives'. As I did so I sensed the fragrance of incense in the area around the altar, in the area where I was preaching. The church was not the kind ever to use incense in worship, so I knew that there could be no natural explanation for this fragrance. I therefore asked if anyone else could smell it and six people near the front of the church said they were aware of it as well. Needless to say, that sign gave us all encouragement to press in and persevere with intercessory prayer. For us it felt like a sign that the Holy Spirit was with us, encouraging and helping us to engage in building an intercessory altar in our lives.

The Fire of Intercession

If this Pauline theology reveals anything, it is the importance of praying in the Spirit rather than in the flesh. If we are to intercede with the mind of Christ, we must allow the Holy Spirit to ignite our hearts so that he can pray in us and through us the prayers of the Ascended Lord. Maybe this is one reason why Paul is so insistent, 'Pray in the Spirit on all occasions' (Ephesians 6:18).

In fulfilling this call we do need to spend some time in silence and listening. So far in this book I have stressed the importance of vocalising our thanksgiving, our praise, our penitence and our petitions. I find it particularly helpful (as an aid to concentration) to do all this out loud. However, more contemplative readers will be asking, 'Doesn't this model of prayer involve an awful lot of talking? Are there not enough words already in our lives? Where's the place of silence and of listening prayer?' If that is a question you have been asking, then let me reassure you by saying that silence and listening are essential before we engage in Spirit-led intercessory prayer. Ecclesiastes 5:1–2 warns us:

> Guard your steps
> when you go to the house of God.
> Go near to listen
> rather than to offer the sacrifice of fools,
> who do not know that they do wrong.
>
> Do not be quick with your mouth,
> do not be hasty in your heart
> to utter anything before God.
> God is in heaven
> and you are on earth,
> so let your words be few.

Before the altar of incense, a contemplative commitment to silence is extremely important before embarking on prayer for others. It is as we invite the Holy Spirit to lead us in our prayers, then wait silently upon his revelation, that we find the direction for our prayers.

So, after a period of silence, I often find that I start to receive a burden for a person or a place, or a series of burdens for people and places. Just occasionally they are hard to miss. David Brainerd, the great eighteenth-century missionary, once had a day which was remarkable for its profound burdens. Jonathan Edwards wrote up his life and diary, and in an entry for 1742, when Brainerd was only 24, we read of three anointings for prayer; one before noon, one in the afternoon, one at night:

In the forenoon, I felt the power of intercession for the advancement of the kingdom of my dear Lord and Saviour in the world; and withal, a most sweet resignation, and even consolation and joy in the thoughts of suffering hardships, distresses, and even death itself, in the promotion of it. In the afternoon, God was with me of a truth. Oh, it was a blessed company indeed! My soul was drawn out very much for the world; I think I had more enlargement for sinners, than for the children of God; though I felt as if I could spend my life in cries for both. Just at night the Lord visited me marvellously in prayer: I think my soul never was in such agony before. I felt no restraint; for the treasures of divine grace were opened to me. I wrestled for absent friends, for the ingathering of souls, and for the children of God in many distant places.[3]

This kind of anointing is, of course, quite exceptional. In general, a burden for prayer is far less overwhelming and, in my experience, a great deal more intuitive. Usually the leading of the Spirit is discerned as we start to catch glimpses of faces in our mind's eye. In between these 'flash photographs', it is helpful to mention the names of the people who are brought to mind, and then to allow the Spirit to do the sighing, the groaning, the speaking, in a language which is not our own. When we do this, we let go of the raft of our own agenda and allow ourselves to enter a stream of divine consciousness – the mind of the Ascended Christ, our Great High Priest.

The Beauty of Intercession

In recent years I have started using the description of the high priest's breastplate (the *choshen harmishpat*) as a great tool for praying for others. In Exodus 28:16–21 we read the instructions that Moses was given by the Lord for the design of this piece of clothing:

> This chestpiece will be made of two folds of cloth, forming a pouch nine inches square. Four rows of gemstones will be attached to it. The first row will contain a red carnelian, a chrysolite, and an emerald. The second row will contain a

turquoise, a sapphire, and a white moonstone. The third row will contain a jacinth, an agate, and an amethyst. The fourth row will contain a beryl, an onyx, and a jasper. All these stones will be set in gold. Each stone will represent one of the tribes of Israel, and the name of that tribe will be engraved on it as though it were a seal.

Personally, I find this an extremely beautiful picture. The names of the 12 tribes of Israel were engraved on precious stones and then held in place over the high priest's chest in four rows of three jewels each. What a great symbol of the loving ministry of intercession. The high priest had the names of those he was called to pray for literally close to his heart. The use of jewels shows how precious, valued and treasured were these individual tribes. It is indeed a beautiful picture.

In the New Testament, Jesus Christ is revealed to be our one and only Great High Priest. Through his death and resurrection he has opened up a new and living way to the Father. Now, at the right hand of God the Father, Jesus Christ exercises a ministry of intercession as the Ascended Lord. He is the Great High Priest and our names are engraved on his heart. We are precious in his eyes, his treasured possession, and he carries us to the Father in passionate cries of intercession. As we read in Hebrews 7:23–25, Jesus is the priest who lives for ever to plead on our behalf:

Another difference is that there were many priests under the old system. When one priest died, another had to take his place. But Jesus remains a priest forever; his priesthood will never end. Therefore he is able, once and forever, to save everyone who comes to God through him. He lives forever to plead with God on their behalf.

As the hymn writer Charity Bancroft once wrote:

Before the throne of God above
I have a strong and perfect plea
A great high priest whose name is love
Who ever lives and breathes for me
My name is graven on his hand
My name is written on his heart

I know that while in heaven he stands
No tongue can bid me thence depart
No tongue can bid me thence depart

Jesus Christ is our Great High Priest, our Mediator and Intercessor. He carries our names to the Father, names that are engraved on his hand and written on his heart. What a beautiful picture!

The Topics of Intercession

I have found it really helpful to imagine wearing this high priest's breastplate myself. We are all of us called to the royal priesthood as believers in Jesus Christ. We can all of us exercise a priestly ministry of prayer. We can all of us come before the Father and minister to him in worship and intercession. Aaron was always to wear the breastplate when he went into the Holy Place. In Exodus 28:29 we read:

> In this way, Aaron will carry the names of the tribes of Israel on the chestpiece over his heart when he goes into the presence of the LORD in the Holy Place. Thus, the LORD will be reminded of his people continually.

Who can we carry before the Father in prayer? Here is a diagram of the breastplate as I see it in my own prayer life, carrying on it the topics of prayer that form a frequent part of my intercessions:

Home

The names of the people I live with are written on my heart and I carry them every day before the Father in intercessory prayer. I begin by praying for my wife Alie, asking the Father for those things that are needed in her life right now, both big and small. I pray for my four children, Philip, Hannah, Johnathan and Sam. Each of them has different needs because each of them is unique in the Lord's eyes. As their father, I bring them before God daily, praying for their education, their health, their friendships, their church activities and their walk with God. In addition, I pray for my home, for the atmosphere in our house, for my marriage, for our parenting skills, for God's protection, and so on.

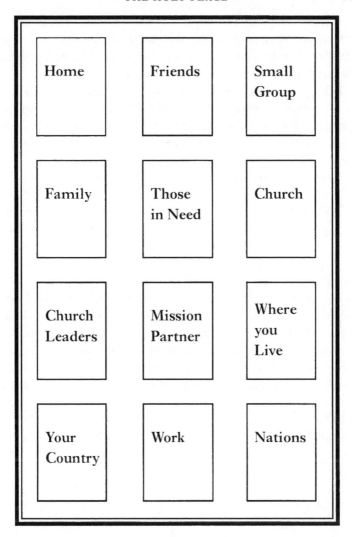

If you are single you may well share a home with others. You can employ exactly the same principles as I do as a husband and a father. You can pray for the house in which you live to be an undisturbed place of rest, a secure home and a dwelling-place of God's *shalom*, God's peace.

Friends
Good friends are a very precious gift. Two that I focus on every day are ministers in their own right. One of them is J. John, a

well-known evangelist in the Church of England. I pray that he
will encounter open doors for the Gospel (Colossians 4:3). I also
pray for his wife Killy and their three boys (especially my godson
Michael), praying specifically for their known needs.

I also pray for an American friend called Marc who is a prophet
to the nations. I pray for the Father's blessing on him, his wife
Kim, and his three children. I ask for the Father's favour for his
work and his finances, and for safety in the frequent travelling he
does.

I base my prayer for friends around 2 John 2:

> Dear friend, I pray that you may enjoy good health and that
> all may go well with you, even as your soul is getting along
> well.

Small group

In our church we encourage every believer to be part of a small
group. My small group is my staff team and their spouses. I meet
every Monday morning with my staff team and once a month in
the evening with the staff and spouses. Their names are written on
my heart too. They are extremely precious to me, they and their
loved ones. I frequently bring them before God in prayer. We use
a staff family prayer list as well. This is something each staff member fills in, enabling all of us to pray specifically for each other and
our families. Jesus prayed for his small group (John 17). We should
too.

Family

By 'family' I mean those that we no longer live with but who are
immediate relatives. I believe as Christians we are called to bring
them before the Father in loving intercessory prayer, even if we do
not get on with them, or are estranged from them. I prayed for over
20 years before my brother Giles made a commitment to Jesus
Christ. He gave his heart to Jesus after being involved in a terrible
car accident. Having been arrested when the police made their
enquiries, he found himself in a prison cell stripped of all the
things he had relied upon for years. He looked up at the ceiling,
saw the name JESUS, and realised there was only one person he
could turn to. That was the turning point in his life. I believe heartfelt intercession played a massive part in that.

The same is true of my twin sister. She came to know Jesus Christ about the same time, several years ago, when she had a scare with a lump. God used that as a wake-up call and today she is a strong Christian living in the USA as a single mum with a beautiful son called Jamie. I prayed that Jamie would also become a Christian and last year I had the privilege of leading him (six years old) to the Lord while I was on a preaching trip in America. I had asked my church members specifically to pray for this before I left, and when I returned they were overjoyed to hear that Jamie had become a Christian.

Those in need

We all have the names of people we love written on our hearts, particularly those who are in great need. We need to keep carrying these loved ones to Jesus on the stretcher of prayer, just like the friends of the paralysed man did in Mark 2. We need to pray for the sick (James 5:14). We especially need to pray for the lost, for those without Jesus (Matthew 9:35–8).

Church

I pray for my local church every day. Often I am surprised by the faces which come into my mind. Just occasionally I sense God's leading to visit someone, or an intuition about what is really happening in someone's marriage or home. Sometimes I pray for wisdom or vision. My main prayer is that St Andrew's Church, and our daughter fellowships, will be filled with the Holy Spirit and see revival in our neighbourhoods. I base my prayer on the tremendous apostolic prayer of Acts 4:23–30.

Church leaders

It is the responsibility of every Christian to pray for their leaders in God. The Bible teaches that we are in a spiritual battle and that the enemy does not fight fair. Often he tries to eliminate leaders by attacking their health, deceiving them theologically, or destroying their family life. One of my favourite verses is Acts 12:5. When Peter, the head of the early Church, is thrown in prison by Herod (who means to execute him), we read, 'But while Peter was in prison, the church prayed very earnestly for him.'

The result of this was that Peter was rescued by an angel. What a reminder of the power there is in praying for church leaders. As

Thomas Watson once wrote, 'the angel fetched Peter out of prison, but it was prayer that fetched the angel!'

Mission partners

Every church should have a heart for mission. As regards mission, we should act locally and think globally, as the saying goes. We have an ever-increasing number of those sent out from us as missionaries, all over the globe. We have a responsibility to pray for them faithfully. We know that prayer for them has a mighty impact. One of our mission partners, in Pakistan, wrote this to me just this morning in an email:

> Today S. drove to collect me from the airport. The situation is quite volatile at the moment and so hence I am not able to use local buses. On the road to the airport suddenly a large group of people were blocking the road and setting fire to vehicles. Several cars in front of S. were set alight. Drivers were leaving their vehicles and running for safety. S. and the man immediately in front managed to get up on the pavement and turn their vehicles round and get away. S. said he just kept saying 'God help me'. Not only was he saved but God was also kind to S. as he knows how much he loves our vehicle and how hard he works to look after it. When he finally arrived at the airport he was pretty shaken, but we travelled back a different route which S. knows because of his many years' experience. Yet again we are so grateful to God and for the prayers of the body.

Where you live

A friend of mine in Norway is the pastor of a thriving church in the city of Bergen on the west coast. He and many of the church leaders in his city have heard a call to unite across denominational boundaries in prayer. Their prayer effort is particularly influenced by the call to pray for civic leaders in 1 Timothy 2:1–4:

> I urge you, first of all, to pray for all people. As you make your requests, plead for God's mercy upon them, and give thanks. Pray this way for kings and all others who are in authority, so that we can live in peace and quietness, in godliness and

dignity. This is good and pleases God our Saviour, for he wants everyone to be saved and to understand the truth.

The results of praying for city leaders have been very positive. There is favour for the churches in the city. The churches themselves have discovered a real vision for blessing their local communities. No wonder the Church is growing in that city.

Praying for the needs of one's local community, praying for blessing on one's neighbourhood, and praying specifically for the needs of civil leaders is an important part of our intercessory ministry as Christians. I often find myself praying for a local school, a pub, a group of people, a housing estate, a particular street, another church, a hospital, whatever. Almost always there is a sense of the Holy Spirit wanting to mediate the healing presence of God to the houses, streets and estates in the community. Sometimes I will receive discernment about the social, structural and spiritual forces which are contributing towards a hitherto unexplained resistance to the Gospel. In any event, I will seek to pray 'Your Kingdom come' in the community where I live.

Your country

We need to make sure our intercessions are not restricted but rather wide-angled in focus. Praying for the royal family, for the government of our nation, for the institutions and agencies which wield power and influence (particularly in the economy and the media), for various professions (especially teachers and the world of education), for topical issues (such as Sunday trading, abortion and so on), is vital. We must allow the Spirit to lead us to pray that the nation in which we live will fulfil its redemptive destiny.

Work colleagues

A church member I know runs a very influential business. He is a Christian who truly believes in the power of prayer. A few years ago he noticed that there were many problems in his workplace so he resolved to come into the large facility where he works and to pray over every desk for every employee, before any of them came to work. The whole atmosphere in the workplace was radically transformed. Peace was restored. People's lives were changed. The business was blessed.

I truly believe that the Holy Spirit wants to help Christians to break down the sacred–secular divide. We tend to operate with a Greek dualism that says God's work is confined to sacred places and sacred times, usually church on Sunday. God wants us to pray in the workplace on Monday just as much as we do in the worship-place on Sunday. God is at work, to use a pun. We need to believe that he is moving in the workplace and start blessing what he wants to do in intercessory prayer. This means writing the names of our work colleagues on our hearts and carrying them to the Father in prayer. It also means praying for those at work who persecute us (Matthew 5:44).

Other nations

My conviction is that God wants to give every praying Christian a burden for at least one specific country or continent. If every pray-ing Christian allowed the Spirit to give them one such burden, the impact on the world would, I believe, be profound and lasting. So permit the Holy Spirit to give you that burden. Do not try to take on too much. The Flash Gordon approach to personal prayer ('Fourteen minutes to save the earth!') usually degenerates into meaningless platitudes. 'God bless us with world peace' is about as vacuous as the answers of a beauty queen in a typical televised pageant. But letting God write the name of a nation on your heart, then carrying the specific needs of that nation to him in prayer, that is truly potent.

One nation I believe we are called to pray for is Israel. We are specifically invited to pray for the city of Jerusalem. As we read in Psalm 122:6–8:

> Pray for the peace of Jerusalem.
> May all who love this city prosper.
> O Jerusalem, may there be peace within your walls
> and prosperity in your palaces.
> For the sake of my family and friends, I will say,
> 'Peace be with you.'

We need to bring the Middle East before the Father in prayer, and specifically the Israeli and Palestinian peoples, asking for the Lord's peace to rest on Jerusalem, the City of Peace.

The Tears of Intercession

For most of us, intercessory prayer will be a ministry just like this: praying through matters relating to home, friends, small groups, family, and so on. This ministry involves silence, in so far as we have to listen to the promptings of the Spirit. It involves speaking, in so far as we pray either in human words or in tongues for others. But it can also require something else as well – tears. As we read in Hebrews 5:7:

> While Jesus was here on earth, he offered prayers and pleadings, with a loud cry and tears, to the one who could deliver him out of death. And God heard his prayers because of his reverence for God.

I remember one Sunday evening in a former church praying for a woman who came to me very troubled. She had entered a season of her life where she seemed to be living with an awful lot of grief. Some of it was about herself and her family. But most of it was for others. Much of her time was spent with a feeling of dereliction for which she felt guilty. As I prayed for her, I began to see a picture developing before my eyes which I shared with her out loud, as it became clearer:

> I can see a great expanse of desert land. It's white with heat and it's very flat. There is absolutely no vegetation there. In the centre of my vision, I can see you. You are standing before an altar made of sand and stone. Your hands are outstretched towards heaven and you are pleading with God on behalf of those whom you know. There is a look of desolation in your face. As you pray, I see streams of tears pouring down your face. As these tears fall to the ground, I see flowers blooming, trees growing, pools of water appearing in every part of the desert. I see the desert turning into a garden. At the same time I see people emerging out of the desert sand, where they have been buried in a kind of living death. The life is returning to their faces. They are smelling the flowers, drinking the water and basking in the shade of the trees. The more your tears flow, the more the land is blessed, and the more the people are healed.

The vision stopped at this point, and as it did, I began to interpret to her what I sensed God might be saying:

> You should not feel guilty about these tears. They are a grace-gift from heaven. The Lord has given you these tears as a form of prayer. Indeed, these tears are the deepest form of prayer. So when you weep, know that you are closer to God than at any other time. You are right in the centre of God's heart, which weeps with compassion for those whose lives are empty and bruised. So let the tears flow. Let the Spirit intercede through you with these tears. And the Lord will turn your grief into joy, your sorrow into dancing.

This incident showed me how precious tears are to God. The prayer of tears is one of the highest forms of worship. If you have been given the tears of intercession, regard it as a privilege. As we read in Isaiah 38:4–5, God loves to respond to the prayer of tears:

> Then the word of the LORD came to Isaiah: 'Go and tell Hezekiah, "This is what the LORD, the God of your father David, says: I have heard your prayer and seen your tears; I will add fifteen years to your life. And I will deliver you and this city from the hand of the king of Assyria. I will defend this city."'

The Mystery of Intercession

We cannot end this chapter on petitionary and intercessory prayer without giving some attention to one of the great mysteries of the Christian life – unanswered prayer. Sometimes we have to say, with complete honesty, that having prayed with the most fervent words and with the most desperate tears, there appears to be no change. The person is not healed. A marriage partner is not provided. Our church is not renewed. Our finances run out. All our pleading at the altar of incense seems to have been to no avail.

There may be a number of reasons for this. Sometimes we have simply not persevered in prayer. We were supposed to knock loudly and persistently on the doors of heaven and instead we only tapped once (Luke 18:1–8). At other times we have underestimated the need for warfare prayer (Ephesians 6:10–18). In other words, we have not seen the level of spiritual oppression in a situation. Instead of hitting enemy tanks with a barrage of constant prayer, we have sought to destroy them with occasional 'arrow prayers'. No wonder little change has occurred!

Sometimes we have simply failed to align ourselves with God's will. In other words, we have asked for the wrong things. We have allowed the desires of our flesh to dictate the how and the what of our prayers. For example, the mother of St Augustine pleaded with God to stop her son from leaving home and travelling to Rome. Yet Augustine left, and on that journey a far greater dream was fulfilled for his mother: Augustine was converted. Later, he wrote about this incident as follows:

> O Lord, in your wisdom, you granted the substance of my mother's desire. You refused the things she prayed for, in order that you might effect in me what she had always wanted. She loved to keep me with her, as mothers are wont to do. In fact, far more than most mothers. But she did not know what joy you were preparing for her as a result of my desertion!

In the final analysis, the Father is completely sovereign when it comes to answering prayer. I have seen God heal the sick. I have also sensed him say, 'This sickness is unto death.' I have seen God say 'yes' to my prayers. I have also heard him say 'not yet' and even 'no'. Sometimes God has answered prayers that have been mere wishful sighs – not even half-prayers in any orthodox sense. At other times he has refused to answer the most poignant pleas. The important thing is not to allow the mystery of God's sovereignty to stop us from praying. God calls us to the table of shewbread and to the golden lampstands. He calls us to petitionary prayer. He also calls us to the altar of incense, to the ministry of intercessory prayer. As priests of the Kingdom, these are essential ministries. God calls us to 'pray constantly' (1 Thessalonians 5:17) and not to give up. As we read in Leviticus 6:13: 'the fire must be kept burning on the altar continuously; it must not go out'. So, in the words of Andrew Murray:

> May God open our eyes to see what the holy ministry of intercession is to which, as his royal priesthood, we have been

set apart. May he give us a large and strong heart to believe what mighty influence our prayers can exert. And may all fear as to our being able to fulfil our vocation vanish as we see Jesus, living ever to pray, living in us to pray, and standing surely for our prayer life.

Prayer

Dear Father, I climb the steps to the Holy Place. Thank you for giving me access to your sanctuary through the death and resurrection of your Son, our Great High Priest.

I pause in the porch out of reverence for your holiness . . .

I now stand before the golden table of shewbread. Thank you for encouraging us to pray, 'Give us this day our daily bread.' Thank you that you are a Father who welcomes our asking, encourages our seeking, answers our knocking. Today I ask you to help me with the following needs that are much on my heart . . .

Lord, I come now to the golden lampstands. I thank you that you want to help me to minister effectively today. Increase in me the spiritual gifts of . . . and draw me closer to yourself, through Jesus.

And now I come to the golden altar of incense. Help me in the silence now to hear what you are saying and to know the mind of Christ . . .

Silence and listening . . .

I pray first of all for my home . . .

I pray for my friends . . .

I pray for our small group . . .

I pray for the family . . .

I pray for those in need . . .

I pray for my church . . .

I pray for my church leaders . . .

I pray for our mission partners . . .

I pray for my community . . .

I pray for my country . . .

I pray for my work colleagues . . .

And I pray for the nations, particularly . . .

And I pray especially for the peace of Jerusalem.

Lord, please answer my prayer.

In Jesus' name.

Amen.

The Holy of Holies

*Prayer ushers us into the Holy of Holies where we
bow before the deepest mysteries of the faith.*
Richard Foster, *Prayer*

The Innermost Sanctuary

We are now nearing the end of our journey into God's presence. We began in Chapter 1 with preparing for the journey by inviting the Holy Spirit. In Chapter 2 we entered the gates of thanksgiving, and looked at the ministry of giving thanks to the Father. In Chapter 3 we proceeded into the court of praise where we explored how to worship the Father and the Son with the prayer of the mind, the prayer of the heart and the prayer of the spirit. In Chapter 4 we paused at the altar of sacrifice and outlined the ministry of confession and repentance. We then entered the Holy Place in Chapter 5, and examined the two ministries of petition (the table of shewbread and the golden lampstands) and intercession (the golden altar of incense). Now we stand before the veil which was used to separate the Holy Place from the Most Holy Place of all.

We read in 1 Kings 6:19 of Solomon's construction of the innermost sanctuary of the Temple:

> Solomon prepared the inner sanctuary within the Temple to set the ark of the covenant of the LORD there. The inner sanctuary was twenty cubits long, twenty wide and twenty high. He overlaid the inside with pure gold, and he also overlaid the altar of cedar.

A few verses later, the narrator describes the interior of the Holy of Holies:

> In the inner sanctuary Solomon made a pair of cherubim of olive wood, each ten cubits high. One wing of the first cherub was five cubits long, and the other wing five cubits – ten cubits from wing tip to wing tip. The second cherub also measured ten cubits, for the two cherubim were identical in size and shape. The height of each cherub was ten cubits. He placed the cherubim inside the innermost room of the Temple, with their wings spread out.

When the great day came and the Temple was completed, the ark of the covenant was brought into the Holy of Holies:

> The priests then brought the ark of the LORD's covenant to its place in the inner sanctuary of the Temple, the Most Holy Place, and put it beneath the cherubim. The cherubim spread their wings over the place of the ark and overshadowed the ark and its carrying poles . . .

As the ark of the covenant was placed in the innermost sanctuary, the cloud of God's glory filled the Holy of Holies:

> When the priests withdrew from the Holy Place, the cloud filled the Temple of the LORD. And the priests could not perform their service because of the cloud, for the glory of the LORD filled his Temple.
>
> 1 Kings 8:6–11

The Place of God's Throne

It is not altogether surprising that the Holy of Holies was seen as the earthly counterpart of God's throne-room in heaven. There are a number of reasons for this. First, the ark of the covenant looked like a throne and was even called 'the cherub throne'. Second, the gold floor and walls were seen as symbolic of God's royalty. The cherubim – celestial angels – were regarded as the concrete counterparts of the angels who surrounded the throne of God in heaven. Third, it was believed that the only source of illumination in the Holy of Holies was the *kabod Yahweh*, the glory of the Lord. While the court of praise was illuminated by the sun, and the Holy Place by candlelight, the innermost sanctuary was believed to be illuminated by the radiant presence of the Lord himself. No wonder the people of God saw the Holy of Holies as a counterpart of the very heart of the heavenly city, where the Lord reigns in majesty. As Jeremiah said, 'A glorious throne set on high from the beginning is the place of our sanctuary' (Jeremiah 17:12). As God says to Ezekiel, from deep within the Temple, 'Son of man, this is the place of my throne and the place for the soles of my feet' (Ezekiel 43:7).

No wonder, then, that the Holy of Holies was seen as the 'throne zone' for the Lord. This was the earthly counterpart of the throne of God in heaven. It pointed to that transcendent realm where the King of Kings was believed to reign in glory, seated between the cherubim, the angels of heaven. As King David put it:

> The LORD reigns,
> let the nations tremble;
> he sits enthroned between the cherubim,
> let the earth shake . . .
> Exalt the LORD our God,
> and worship at his footstool;
> he is holy.
>
> Psalm 99:1, 5

The greatest vision of the throne zone of heaven was given to the Apostle John in the Book of Revelation. As he sat in chains in his prison cell on the penal colony of Patmos, he was caught up in the Holy Spirit and allowed to look through an open door in heaven. What he sees looks very like the earthly Temple. He describes a seven-branched *menorah* (1:12; 4:5), an altar where incense is offered (5:8; 6:9; 8:3–5), a great sea of crystal before the throne (reminiscent of the bronze sea, 4:6) and the ark of the covenant (11:19). The furniture of the throne-room of heaven looks very like the furniture of the Temple in Jerusalem.

The focal point of everything in John's heavenly vision is the throne of God, which is again reminiscent of the cherub throne in the Holy of Holies. John portrays this part of heaven in the most majestic terms. In Revelation chapters 4 and 5 we are given a brief but awesome glimpse of the worship of God which has been taking place since the very beginning of time, and which will go on for eternity.

The Book of Revelation is extremely pertinent for our final ministry as priests of the Kingdom of God. Once we enter through the veil and kneel in the Holy of Holies, we are in the presence of the One who was, who is, who is to come, the Almighty (1:8). After all our thanking, praising, confessing, petitioning and interceding, we pause now to worship God in all his infinite glory. Here we come before the throne of God and worship at his footstool. Here we enjoy a vital spiritual discipline: beholding the throne in devotional prayer.[1]

Transcendence and Immanence

The discipline of beholding the throne involves a fixed attention upon the royal majesty of God. This is a much-needed discipline because there is always a danger that we can lose touch with the transcendence of God. The Chambers Dictionary defines the word 'transcendent' as 'superior or supreme in excellence'. It defines the verb 'transcend' as 'to rise above' and 'to pass or lie beyond the limit of'. When I speak of the transcendence of God I mean his super-eminent otherness. I mean that aspect of his being which is mysterious, fearful, beyond our limited understanding.

Here we have much to learn from our brothers and sisters in the Eastern Orthodox Church. In Orthodox worship there is a great deal of emphasis upon the Holy Spirit and upon the nearness of God. But a primary theme of Orthodox theology is also the infinite majesty and transcendence of God – as One who lies beyond our understanding and our language. As Bishop Kallistos of Diokleia writes:

> We approach the living God 'in fear and trembling', 'in love and awe'. Negative or apophatic language is used to underline the divine transcendence: God's power is 'indescribable' and his goodness 'unutterable'; 'your glory cannot be approached . . . no one has ever seen you nor is able to see you . . . who alone are holy, immeasurable and beyond human expression . . . incomprehensible in being'. Such language, so far from being an empty formality, expresses a vivid, inescapable conviction pervading all Orthodox theology.[2]

The conviction of the Orthodox Christian is therefore this: that God is on the one hand the core of everything, closer to us than our own heart. That is why an Orthodox service will begin with an invocation and invitation of the Holy Spirit, who is 'everywhere present and filling all things'. On the other hand, God is seen by Orthodox Christians as transcendent to or beyond us. So the same service will contain prayers which focus upon the transcendence of God:

> Around your throne in heaven
> angelic powers exalt you

with ceaseless hymns
and unending songs of praise;
so may your praise be ever on our lips
that we may proclaim
the greatness of your holy Name.[3]

Orthodox spirituality has a healthy regard for the transcendence of God, without sacrificing his immanence or nearness.

In Pentecostal spirituality it is exactly the opposite. Pentecostal and Charismatic Christians have a healthy regard for the immanence of God without sacrificing his transcendence or otherness. 'Immanence' refers to the indwelling, empowering presence of God. For Pentecostals and Charismatics, God is with us in power and in person, through the dynamic presence of his Spirit. This is an experiential reality.

The Bible shows that God is indeed immanent. With the birth of Jesus, God has truly become present with us. He is 'Immanuel', 'God with us'. With the outpouring of the Holy Spirit at Pentecost, things have gone one stage further. For Christians it is true that God is not only 'with us' but 'in us'. The presence of the Holy Spirit in our lives is the immanence of Almighty God. In Pentecostal and Charismatic theology, the emphasis therefore falls on God's immanence (without sacrificing his transcendence). As John McKay has written:

> No charismatic would feel at home with the kind of biblical interpretation that speaks simply of 'the supernatural', 'the divine', 'the numinous', 'the transcendent', or that would seek to interpret all in terms of purely human understanding, scientific thought, or philosophy. To him God is Father, Lord and King, and is very near and very personal.[4]

The God who is Good but not Safe

Of course, it is a case of both/and, not either/or. A balanced theological perspective holds together a sense of God's transcendent otherness and his immanent nearness. The truly biblical theologian knows on the one hand that God is the Lord of the Universe and the High King of Heaven, who reigns in radiant majesty and unapproachable light. On the other hand, the same theologian also recognises that God is the perfect Father who longs for intimacy with his children, and who has made such a relationship possible through the amazing sacrifice of his Son and the continuing work of the Holy Spirit – the fire of the Father's love, shed abroad in our hearts. The true theologian knows that it is not either transcendence *or* immanence, it is both transcendence *and* immanence.

In C. S. Lewis' story, *The Lion, the Witch and the Wardrobe*, there is a very revealing exchange between two girls and a Mr and Mrs Beaver. The subject of their conversation is Aslan, a lion who, in Lewis' tale, symbolises the Son of God:

> 'Is – is he a man?' asked Lucy.
>
> 'Aslan a man!' said Mr Beaver sternly. 'Certainly not. I tell you he is the King of the wood and the son of the great Emperor-Beyond-the-Sea. Don't you know who is the King of Beasts? Aslan is a lion – *the* lion, the great Lion.'
>
> 'Ooh!' said Susan, 'I'd thought he was a man. Is he – quite safe? I shall feel rather nervous about meeting a lion.'
>
> 'That you will, dearie, and no mistake', said Mrs Beaver.
>
> 'If there's anyone who can appear before Aslan without their knees knocking, they're either braver than most or else just silly.'
>
> 'Then he isn't safe?' said Lucy.
>
> 'Safe?' said Mr Beaver. 'Don't you hear what Mrs Beaver tells you? Who said anything about safe? Course he isn't safe. But he's good. He's the King, I tell you.'[5]

What I admire about this conversation is the idea that Aslan is good but not necessarily safe. This is a perfect description of God. In the New Testament, there are times when God does not seem to be altogether safe and predictable. For instance, in the Acts of the Apostles we see a God who lifts his Son Jesus into heaven (Acts 1), who shakes buildings and descends on people with tongues of fire (Acts 2), who heals a man crippled from birth (Acts 3), who strikes down those who hold back from giving their all financially (Acts 5), and so on. Who would not fear such an awesome God?

The first recorded prayer of the Spirit-filled believers in Acts 4:23–30 shows how they appreciated this sense of God's otherness. Their prayer begins with the words, 'Sovereign Lord'. The Greek word for 'Sovereign Lord' is *despota* from which we get 'despot'. A despot is someone with absolute power, usually a tyrant! By using the word *despota*, the believers in Jerusalem were expressing their respect for God, the King of Creation (v. 24), the Lord of History (vv. 25–8) and the Head of the Church (vv. 29–30). They were expressing their faith in a God who is good, but not necessarily safe.

At the same time, the earliest Christians also knew that Jesus came to reveal that the Creator of the Universe is the most loving Father. The fatherhood of God is in fact the premier message of Jesus' teaching, along with the message of the Kingdom of God. Jesus alone, in the context of the world religions, reveals that the One who called the galaxies into being and threw stars into space is actually a Father who loves us dearly (John 16:27). Only Jesus shows us that God is like this. As Michael Green writes:

> Only Jesus fully understands God the Father. Great people have discovered and taught many things about God. Nobody has known him with the intimacy of Jesus, who could call him Abba, 'Dear Daddy'.

Jesus came to draw us into that same intimate union with the Father that he himself enjoyed. The first Christians knew that too!

While Aslan may not be entirely safe (he is a lion after all!), we must not forget that he is also good. He may roar at his enemies and throw them into confusion. But he also allows his friends – those who will become like children before him – to come near and embrace him. He is at the same time both dangerously mighty and incomparably affectionate.

The King who is a Father

How are we to hold these two things together? In beholding the throne of God in prayer, there are two attendant dangers. On the one hand we can become so fixated on God's otherness that we lose any sense of his intimate embrace. On the other hand we can become so fixated on his nearness that we lose any sense of his royal transcendence. The first danger is the danger of constructing a God-image in which we become alienated from the object of our worship. The second danger is the danger of constructing a

God-image in which we become over-familiar with the object of our worship.

At this point I would like to offer a picture that may help us in getting the balance right between God's transcendence (God as transcendent King) and his immanence (God as affectionate Father) in our approach to the Lord in the throne-room:

> The small boy, not quite three years old, skipped down the imposing corridors. Armed servicemen, the best of the best, took no notice of the child who ran past their assigned posts. The boy passed several staff members on his way, who likewise took little notice except for an occasional smile. Passing a secretary's desk, the little boy did not acknowledge her wave, intent as he was on his goal. In front of the door stood another armed sentry. But the guard made no movement to hinder the progress of the child who opened the door and went inside. With a grin, the boy ran across the carpet of the Oval Office and climbed into the lap of the most powerful man in the world. Influential cabinet members had to wait to continue their discussion as President John F. Kennedy and his son John-John exchanged good morning hugs and kisses.[6]

I offer this as a parable because I believe it holds two truths in balance as far as our approach to God is concerned. Prayer is communication with the High King of Heaven, the most powerful person in the universe. But a major key to this union is to understand that the King is also our Heavenly Father. Jesus, in the prayer that he taught his disciples, asked us to begin our devotions with the words 'Our Father in heaven'. Jesus came to reconcile us to the Father. We were estranged from our Father in heaven, living as spiritual orphans in the cosmos. But Jesus Christ died on the Cross and opened up the new and living way to the Father – a way far superior to the sacrifices in the old covenant era. Thanks to Calvary, we can all enter through the torn veil into the Most Holy Place of the King's presence. But the King is also a Dad, the most perfect Father.

Every follower of Jesus Christ has this kind of unhindered and free access to the Father. As Paul says in Ephesians 2:18, 'through him [Jesus] we both [Gentile and Jew] have *access* to the Father by one Spirit'. Thanks to what Jesus Christ has done on the Cross, we can enter into the Most Holy Place of the Father's presence. As we read in Hebrews 4:14–16:

> Therefore, since we have a great high priest who has gone through the heavens, Jesus the Son of God, let us hold firmly to the faith we profess. For we do not have a high priest who is unable to sympathize with our weaknesses, but we have one who has been tempted in every way, just as we are – yet was without sin. Let us then approach the throne of grace with confidence, so that we may receive mercy and find grace to help us in our time of need.

In the Holy of Holies, we can spend time resting and rejoicing in the presence of the King who is also a Dad. Even though this is the place of God's throne, it is a place where we are welcome, because of what the Lord Jesus has done. What a mystery and what a marvel! The High King of Heaven is a Father who delights to be with us. We are his adopted sons and daughters. We can approach him boldly and freely enjoy his affections.

One of my favourite photographs of the twentieth century shows John F. Kennedy Jr ('John-John') playing in the Oval Office as a toddler. His father – the President of the United States – is sitting at the Resolute Desk, clearly working on history-making issues. His little boy is crawling through the carefully designed knee-hole in the front of the desk, peeking out in time to be caught on camera.

What a picture of our relationship with God! God is the High King of heaven and also a loving Father who welcomes us into his presence, saying, 'If you will become like a little child then you can enter the Kingdom.' Our Heavenly Father is longing for us to enter into the pleasure of knowing him as children know their Father. As we read in Psalm 68:5: 'A father to the fatherless, a defender of widows, is God in his holy dwelling' (New International Version).

As we come now to the final stage of our journey in prayer, we need to remember that God is our King but he is also our Dad. Yes, we behold the throne in the Most Holy Place, and this reminds us that God is indeed royal, majestic, awesome and other. At the same time we remember that the Ascended Lord Jesus refers to this as 'my Father's throne' (Revelation 3:22). This is the place where we find our Father. Prayer is ultimately an audience with the King of Kings, but we should not forget that it is also time spent with the Father of Lights. As Billy Graham once said:

> Prayer to God is like a child's conversation with his Father. Avail yourself of the greatest privilege this side of heaven. Jesus Christ died to make this communication with the Father possible.

Beholding the Throne in Prayer

Having provided this very necessary theological backdrop, we come now to the fifth and final stage of prayer using the Temple model.

In this last stage of prayer, we pause at the entrance to the Holy of Holies. Traditionally, a great ornamented veil separated the Holy Place from the Most Holy Place. Once every year – at *Yom Kippur*, the Day of Atonement – the Jewish high priest was permitted to enter through the veil to atone for the sins of the people. Under the new covenant, of course, all this has changed: the death of Jesus has meant that all those who trust in Christ can enter the Most Holy Place of God's presence. As a result of Calvary, the veil in the Temple has been torn in two, thereby leaving the entrance to the heart of God wide open for those who believe and trust in Christ. This means that we can have access to the innermost sanctuary; we can walk with reverence into the presence of the King of Kings who is also our Heavenly Father.

What we do when we enter the innermost sanctuary is to meditate on the throne of God described in Revelation 4—5. This form of meditation is a concentrated and imaginative focus upon God's majesty as described in this passage. It is a spiritual discipline which is commanded in Scripture. That is why, in Colossians 3:1–3, Paul tells his readers:

> Since, then, you have been raised with Christ, set your hearts on things above, where Christ is seated at the right hand of God. Set your minds on things above, not on earthly things. For you died, and your life is now hidden with Christ in God.

How do we set our hearts and minds on the throne above? Here I want to describe the key practice of meditating on the throne of God. This in essence involves a slow reading of Revelation 4—5 in which we allow each statement to impact us so that we can respond in either silent or vocal worship.

It needs to be said at the outset that this is not an easy discipline to master. In reading the Bible we have become hopelessly handicapped by the principles of the Enlightenment. For centuries we have been reading the Scriptures for information, not for transformation. In other words, we have been reading them as a source of historical data rather than as the Word of God which transforms us. Furthermore, we have been reading the Bible from a perspective of detachment rather than from a perspective of participation. In other words, we have learnt to stand above the text like a scientist examining a cell under a microscope. We have lost the art of being able to enter into the world of the text, to feel the experiences it describes, to identify with the characters depicted, to respond to the signals it elicits. A meditative approach to the Bible is altogether different. It requires us to be formed and not just informed. It also requires total participation in the world of the text. Detachment will not do. We must be prepared to enter into the symbolic universe of the Bible, however strange some of those symbols may seem to us today.

In relation to Revelation 4—5, a meditative reading requires us to take each phrase of the chapter, accepting it as a true insight into the heavenly realm, and to allow it to evoke a devotional response from our hearts.

In the following pages, we will take phrases from Revelation 4—5 and highlight some of the affective responses which they might encourage as a result of a meditative reading.

These are suggestions for responding to John's vision of the throne zone of heaven. They are not in any way meant to be prescriptive.

After this I looked

In the Ignatian tradition of meditating on Scripture, the human senses play a significant part in the reading process. We are encouraged to smell, to taste, to touch, to hear, and above all to see what the Scriptures describe. The word 'looked' in the opening statement of Revelation 4 alerts us straight away to the need to open the eyes of our imagination to the realities being presented. What is about to follow is of a very visual nature. We must therefore activate our imaginations to look with love upon the heavenly realities of John's vision.

Notice that the writer says, 'I looked'. There are a number of things that are significant here. First of all, we should note that this is in the past tense. St John says, 'I looked', not 'I see'. In order for us to register the content of this scripture as a reality in our own experience, we must turn what was past tense for St John into a present tense. From now on I will therefore be referring to the content of Revelation 4 in the present tense.

Secondly, we need to notice the little word 'I' in 'I looked'. St John is emphasising that the vision was originally a personal experience. This again is important for meditative reading. In meditating upon Revelation 4, it is important to personalise the scripture; that is, to see the vision as a direct experience for us now. This means that from now on I shall be referring to my own experience as I gaze upon the majesty of God.

There before me is an open door

Doors are powerful symbols. In John 10:7, Jesus says, 'I am the door.' In Revelation 3:20, Jesus says, 'Behold! I stand at the door and knock.' Clearly a threshold must be crossed if I am to participate in the heavenly word of Revelation 4.

Entering the open door in heaven is the ultimate liminal experience. The word 'liminal' comes from the Latin *limen* meaning 'a threshold'. As I pass through the open door in heaven I see myself at the threshold of eternity. I prepare myself for what Thérèse of Lisieux called 'dreaming of heaven'.[7]

As I start to meditate on this truth, I begin to wonder at the generosity of the Father. It is an open door to eternity. The door is open wide, not shut. There is a sense of divine invitation and welcome here. My Father says, 'Come up here, my child.' I respond by walking into what George Ladd called 'the presence of the future'.[8]

At once I am in the Spirit

As soon as I hear these words, I am 'in the Spirit'. Here I pause and reflect on what it means to be 'in the Spirit' in prayer. I remember that the promise of Scripture is that in prayer I am lifted up by the

Spirit into the presence of the Ascended Christ. Paul says in Romans 8:26 that we do not know how to pray because we are weak. However, the Holy Spirit helps us in our weakness and intercedes within us. More than that, the Holy Spirit joins our prayer to the prayer of Jesus before the throne of the Father.

Whether I feel it or not, the fact is I am right now elevated from the frailty of my humanity into the unending dialogue of prayer between the Son and the Father in heaven. According to Romans 8, I am lifted up out of my weakness. I am gathered up into the life of the Holy Trinity – joined by the Holy Spirit to the perfect worship and intercession of the Son in the presence of the Father.

There before me is a throne in heaven

The first sight I see is God's throne. It is a magnificent throne, a huge throne which seems to function as a primary source of light. I cannot make out the form of God upon this throne because light seems to be pouring out of the very centre of it. It is an awesome sight, in many ways so far beyond anything that is describable. Perhaps that is why St John is unusually sparse with his words. All he says is that there is a throne in heaven. All I can do is recognise that I am in the presence of royalty. I am in the presence of the *Pantokrator*, the Almighty, the One who is Lord of History and King of Creation; the One before whom every knee must one day bow.

And there is someone sitting on it

How I admire the reticence of St John! He is so overawed by what he sees that he cannot even name God. He describes God as 'someone sitting on the throne'. He does the same thing in Revelation 4:3 ('the one who sat there'); 4:9 ('him who sits on the throne'); 4:10 ('him who sits on the throne'); 5:1 ('him who sat on the throne'); and 5:7 ('him who sat on the throne'). Although God has given us names for himself, I must use them with enormous respect and honour. He is my Father, yes, but he is also the One who is seated on the throne of heaven.

The One who sits there has the appearance of jasper and carnelian

God is revealed in glorious technicolour here, not in grey hues or a mundane and boring black and white. In fact, I love the exotic colours emanating from the throne of God. Jasper is an opaque quartz, a precious stone. Carnelian is a translucent red stone. Jasper and carnelian are the prismatic colours through which the unapproachable light of God's glory is reflected (1 Timothy 6:16).

As I worship at the Father's footstool, I know that he sees me in the best possible light. To quote Eugene Petersen, 'Lives that have been defaced by sin into blurred charcoal outlines are now seen in their true colours. Every faded tint and wavering line is restored to original sharpness and hue.'⁹ I bathe in the healing light of the Father's acceptance.

A rainbow, resembling an emerald, encircles the throne
I spend a few moments looking above the throne, where a velvety-green rainbow glows like a huge halo. I worship my Father in the silence of true appreciation and gratitude because the rainbow is a sign of God's mercy. I recall God's words in Genesis 9:12–16, and hear them as personally addressing me:

> This is the sign of the covenant I am making between me and you and every living creature with you, a covenant for all generations to come: I have set my rainbow in the clouds, and it will be the sign of the covenant between me and the earth. Whenever I bring clouds over the earth and the rainbow appears in the clouds, I will remember my covenant between me and you and all living creatures of every kind. Never again will the waters become a flood to destroy all life. Whenever the rainbow appears in the clouds, I will see it and remember the everlasting covenant between God and all living creatures of every kind on the earth.

The emerald rainbow encircling God's throne is a reminder that my heavenly Father accepts me because of his mercy revealed in Christ Jesus. Jesus has drunk from the cup of God's wrath. Therefore I know the truth of Hebrews 4:16, that I may approach the throne of grace with confidence in order to receive mercy and find grace to help me in every hour of need. How I thank God that his throne is a place of mercy, not of judgement!

Surrounding the throne are 24 other thrones

As my eyes shift from what I can see above the throne, I see there are 24 other thrones around the royal throne. On these thrones sit 24 elders. Twelve are the representatives of the old covenant, the original leaders of the 12 tribes of Israel. The other 12 are the representatives of the new covenant, the 12 apostles. These elders are dressed in white with crowns of gold upon their heads. As I look at them, I remember the first line of a hymn: 'O, welcome all ye noble saints of old'. I recall that I am surrounded by a great crowd of witnesses.

From the throne come flashes of lightning, rumblings and peals of thunder

From seeing I turn to hearing. The lightning and thunder are deafening. I am only feet away from the throne from which they are exploding. I have to put my hands over my ears. I sense the awesome power of God as the lightning spears its way from the throne across the vast expanse of heaven. I sense the greatness of God as I hear the thunder crash around me. I have a sense of my vulnerability, my mortality and my finitude.

Before the throne seven lamps are blazing . . . and there is what looks like a sea of glass, clear as crystal

But then I see something strange. After the tremendous movement and energy of the thunder and the lightning comes the still calm of the heavenly counterparts of the *menorah* and the brazen sea. I gaze upon the burning flames in the seven golden candlesticks and ask the Spirit to minister revelation. I stand before the crystal sea and ask the Spirit to minister rest. I breathe in the air of heaven, and listen to the quietest hint of wave upon shore. In a moment of heavenly stasis, I rest in the presence of the King of Kings.

Before the throne are four living creatures

Suddenly I see them, four strange creatures stationed around the centre of the Father's royal throne. John says that the first of these is like a lion, the second is like an ox, the third is like a man, the fourth is like a flying eagle. They are covered with eyes and are all able to fly. Indeed, they are actually flying just above the throne of God, and above the 24 thrones surrounding God's throne.

I see four groups of beings around the throne: first of all, the four living creatures; then the 24 elders; then the 'many angels, numbering thousands upon thousands, and ten thousand times ten thousand' (Revelation 5:11); and finally, 'every creature in heaven and on earth and under the earth and on the sea'.

I see these as ever-increasing circles of praise. At the very centre of this praise is the Royal Father upon his throne. Then there are the four living creatures directly around and above the throne. After that are the 24 elders. Following them are the myriads of angels. Following them is the whole of creation.

The four living creatures are, in a strange sense, a comfort to me. They tell me that I, and indeed the whole of creation, am welcome in the throne zone of heaven. The whole of the universe is called to the throne to worship the King. As Eugene Petersen puts it:

> The act of worship gathers into its centring rituals and harmonizing rhythms every aspect of creation. Worship does not divide the spiritual from the natural, it coordinates them. Nature and supernature, creation and covenant, elders and animals are all gathered. Worship that scorns creation is impoverished. The rabble of creation 'red in tooth and claw' comes to order before the throne and finds itself more itself: each creature is alert (full of eyes) and soaring (six wings). In George Herbert's words: 'All creatures of my God and King, lift up your voice and sing!'[10]

Day and night, they never stop saying, 'Holy, holy, holy!'
The noise of the thunder fades and a new sound is heard – the sound of the four living creatures worshipping God. Now I begin to notice the variety of worship around God's throne. The four living creatures and the 24 elders declare rather than sing their praises. Their declarations are united statements of adoration of God the Holy One. The four living creatures start this worship with the words, 'Holy, holy, holy is the Lord Almighty, who was, and is, and is to come.' As soon as the 24 elders hear this, they fall down and proclaim:

You are worthy, our Lord and God,
to receive glory and honour and power,
for you created all things,
and by your will they were created and have their being.

This is worship which is said, not sung. It is worship addressed to
God the Creator.

The next three outbursts of worship are different. They are all
in the form of song, and they follow directly after the appearance
of the Lamb of God in Revelation 5:1–7. When the four living
creatures and the 24 elders understand that Jesus, the Lamb of
God, is the only one in heaven and on earth worthy enough to
receive the scroll, they join forces to sing a spontaneous new song:

You are worthy to take the scroll
and to open its seals,
because you were slain,
and with your blood
you purchased men for God
from every tribe and language
and people and nation.
You have made them to be a kingdom
and priests to serve our God,
and they will reign on the earth.

As soon as the angels hear this song, they in turn sing their own
song in a loud voice:

Worthy is the Lamb, who was slain,
to receive power and wealth
and wisdom and strength
and honour and glory and praise!

These two songs in Revelation 5 are addressed to Jesus, the Lamb
of God. If the first two songs address God the Creator, the second
two address God the Redeemer. In the last song, however, both the
Father who reigns on the throne, and the Son who is at the centre
of the throne, are honoured and adored in one and the same song.

Now it is the turn of the whole of creation to sing a final, great doxology:

> To him who sits on the throne
> and to the Lamb
> be praise and honour and glory and power,
> for ever and ever!

In all of this, I cannot help noticing that the worship of the creatures, the elders and the angels is about Calvary. I see Jesus, 'a Lamb, looking as if it had been slain, standing in the centre of the throne, encircled by the four living creatures and the elders'. When the Lamb of God appears, the four living creatures and the 24 elders worship him for having purchased people for God from every tribe and language and people and nation. They shout 'Worthy is the Lamb, who was slain.' Calvary is therefore the central cause of sung worship in heaven:

> Crown him the Lord of love;
> Behold his hands and side,
> Those wounds yet visible above
> In beauty glorified:
> No angel in the sky
> Can fully bear that sight,
> But downward bends his burning eye
> At mysteries so bright.

From Meditation to Contemplation

Beholding the throne is an exercise that requires discipline and hard work. We start with Revelation 4—5 open before us and we go through it verse by verse. Gradually the passage becomes so familiar to us that we no longer need our Bibles in front of us. Instead we work our way through the vision with the help of both our memory and our imagination. Once we have got this far, we have made the transition from meditation to contemplation. Meditation is a fixed attention on a passage. Contemplation is a devotional awareness of God which is not tied to a biblical text or a visible object. Contemplation is pure, unaided adoration.

After weeks of reading we therefore start to practise Spirit-led recollection. This is where the adventure begins. Many people at this stage begin to find that beholding the throne is something which they look forward to immensely. One friend of mine who heard me speak on this subject told me that it is this form of prayer which he enjoys most. It has proved an invaluable source of personal refreshment and renewal for him. Every time is different. When he is feeling in need of encouragement, he stops and contemplates the emerald rainbow, and reminds himself of God's mercy. At other times when he is feeling frail, he pauses at the throne, imagining the thunder and lightning, and remembers God's power. Sometimes when he is feeling tired and overworked, he pictures the sea of glass, and drinks in the stillness where God is.

In teaching this discipline to his church, this friend told me that he likens it to shopping. When we go shopping, we walk through the streets and the arcades and stop at those shops which catch our attention. We do not attempt to go into every shop which we pass and browse there. The same is true for beholding the throne in prayer. Once we have become familiar with the passage, the point is not to try and spend a lot of time focusing on each aspect of the vision. Rather, we should allow the Spirit to show us which part of this scripture will most nourish us today.

While I would want to avoid any connotations of 'consumerism' in beholding the throne of God, I do find this idea of shopping a helpful analogy. It makes our priestly ministry in the Holy of Holies a more accessible and a less daunting one. We do not have to cover everything in a systematic way. We do not have to feel obliged to spend time covering every tiny detail. We can be led by the Holy Spirit to choose and to focus on what is relevant to us at any given moment.

From Contemplation to Vision

Beholding the Lord in prayer therefore requires work and discipline. After a while, meditation turns to contemplation. If we are really blessed, there may come a time when contemplation turns to vision.

What happens when we move on from a contemplative and anointed *anamnesis* or remembrance to an actual vision of heaven? Here we move from the symbols themselves to the realities to which they point. We move from the signifiers to their signified. It is a very rare privilege, and not everyone will experience it this side of eternity. But just occasionally, God will lead someone who regularly practises this discipline into the highest form of divine union which a human being can attain: a vision of some aspect of the heavenly realm.

A member of a former church was once receiving the ministry of healing prayer. She had heard my teaching on beholding the throne and had started to develop the practice of 'dreaming of heaven'. As she was being prayed for she saw the following:

> It came to me early in the ministry prayers. My eyes were closed, and ten feet in front of me appeared a large lion, walking from left to right. His face didn't leave mine. He kept looking at me as he proudly, triumphantly, powerfully and majestically walked to and fro. I was overwhelmed by a sense of his royal dignity. I felt safe and relaxed. This was Jesus, Immanuel, God with us.
>
> The next thing I noticed were three winged animals about ten feet above him, in the two o'clock position (at the time, I saw them as seraphs). I noticed the wings more than anything. I couldn't see their bodies except to say that they were rounded at the edges. They only moved very slightly. They appeared weightless. The lion was a glorious golden colour with a wonderfully long mane. Apart from the lion and the three strange animals, the rest seemed to be dark, especially the background.
>
> Next, I heard a distant trumpet sound. I couldn't pick out any notes (it was a major key, however). Somehow I felt that there were three instruments playing. The music seemed to be saying, 'Praise him! Praise him!' It all felt regal, but welcoming too!
>
> This vision of Jesus is extremely important to me and I'll never forget it. I still see a vision of the lion occasionally when in prayer.

This woman had moved from meditation to contemplation, and from contemplation to vision. Having filled her mind with heavenly realities, she was ready to be anointed with a vision of the Lion of Judah before the throne.

Maybe you and I will one day have this privilege of true mystical union as well.

The Door to Eternity

So why is it important to have a go at beholding the throne of God in prayer? One of the greatest reasons for attempting this form of prayer is the simple fact that it gives us a glimpse of our eternal destiny. A daily ministry of 'dreaming of heaven' is not a form of escapism in which we become so heavenly-minded that we are no earthly use, as the saying goes. It is a way of facing the reality of our mortality. As King David put it:

> You have made my days a mere handbreadth;
> the span of my years is as nothing before you.
> Each man's life is but a breath.
>
> Psalm 39:5

Beholding the throne is not only a means of helping us to confront our mortality and our finitude, it is also a way of preparing us for heaven. I find in my ministry that there are few people today who know what the Bible says about heaven. Is it any surprise, then, that our society is so hopeless and pessimistic? If the Church cannot be certain about the nature of its ultimate future, then who can?

The virtue of a daily focus on the throne of God is that it constantly reminds us of what will happen to us after God has raised us from the sleep of death on the last day. From that day onwards, we will be worshipping with that great cloud of witnesses gathered in circles of praise around God's throne. This means that every time we enter the Most Holy Place to behold the Lord we are making ready for our eternal home, where we will see endless theophanies which will feel more real than reality.

New Heaven, New Earth

Nothing reminded me more powerfully of this need to fix our hearts on eternity than the death of the daughter of a Christian friend. On a bank holiday Monday some years ago, I received a phone call. My friend Duncan just uttered the words, 'Ericka's dead.' I put down the phone immediately and hurried around to his house. When I arrived there, Ericka was lying dead in her mother's arms. She was only twelve years old.

Duncan and I sat on the bed for a long time in silence. Ericka looked peaceful after her long struggle with disease. Even so, all we could do was weep quietly. But then something very powerful happened. Helen, Ericka's mother, held her daughter close and shut her eyes. As she did so, beautiful words of hope started to flow from her mouth:

> Then I saw a new heaven and a new earth, for the first heaven and the first earth had passed away, and there was no longer any sea. I saw the Holy City, the new Jerusalem, coming down out of heaven from God, prepared as a bride beautifully dressed for her husband. And I heard a loud voice from the throne saying, 'Now the dwelling of God is with men, and he will live with them. They will be his people and God himself will be with them and be their God. He will wipe every tear from their eyes. There will be no more death or mourning or crying or pain, for the old order of things has passed away.'

These words from Revelation 21 changed the whole atmosphere of the bedroom. Although they did not remove the sense of loss, they opened up a horizon of hope where before there was only dereliction. They helped us to stand with Ericka, just for a moment, on the threshold of a great eternity.

Spend time in the Most Holy Place, contemplating the throne of God, preparing for heaven. Whenever you behold the Lord in prayer, you enter an atmosphere of worship which is not wholly of this world. You enter an atmosphere which is thick with angels. That is why it is important to spend time entering the door to eternity in prayer. Every time you cross this threshold, you will be able to say with Jacob, 'How awesome is this place! This is none other than the house of God, and this is the gate of heaven' (Genesis 28:17).

Reviewing the Journey

When you have completed 95 per cent of your journey, you are still only half way there.

Japanese proverb

God said to the people of Israel, 'You will be for me a kingdom of priests and a holy nation' (Exodus 19:6). This book has been an attempt to give both a theological and a practical framework for living out our royal priesthood in daily prayer, using the Temple model as a way of going deeper into the Father's presence.

In Chapter 1 I showed how prayer must begin with inviting the Holy Spirit to come and fill us with the fire of his love. Just as the Temple in Jerusalem was filled with the cloud of God's glory, so we need to welcome the presence of God into the Temple model of prayer. Otherwise it will be all form and no fire.

In Chapter 2 I looked at the importance of giving thanks. The Bible tells us to enter his gates with thanksgiving. 'Thanks' is one of our best words; it is the password into the Lord's presence. Spending time thanking the Father for his goodness releases even more of his fatherly goodness into our lives. God is a Father whose heart expands with even greater generosity every time we spontaneously give him thanks. Thanking God is the best place to begin our journey into his presence, after welcoming the person of the Holy Spirit.

In Chapter 3 we moved on from the gates of thanksgiving to the court of praise. If thanking God means focusing on what he has done, praising God means focusing on who he is. In the court of praise we bring the sacrifice of our adoration, particularly lifting up the person of Jesus in our worship, praying in the light of his many names, giving him all the glory as we magnify who he is.

In Chapter 4 we came to the altar of sacrifice. In the old covenant this was a bronze altar. Today, in the new covenant, it is the Cross of Christ. Here we come and stand before the Cross on which the Prince of Glory died. Just as in the Old Testament sin was dealt with ruthlessly at this altar, so now, in the New Testament era, we resolve to treat our sins with finality, not frivolity. Here then is the place to be washed and sanctified by the blood of Christ and the cleansing streams of the Holy Spirit before we climb the steps into the Holy Place.

In Chapter 5 we entered the sanctuary, pausing at the table of shewbread in order to engage in petitionary prayer – prayer, in other words, for our own personal needs. Jesus encouraged us to pray, 'Give us this day our daily bread.' The Father is concerned about the practical needs of our lives. As Henry Ward Beecher once said:

> Prayer covers the whole of a person's life. There is no thought, feeling, yearning or desire, however low, trifling, or vulgar, we may deem it, which, if it affects our real interest or happiness, we may not lay before God and be sure of sympathy. His nature is such that our often coming does not tire him. The whole burden of the whole life of every person may be rolled onto God and not weary him, though it has wearied the person.

The Father is interested in our practical needs, and he is also concerned about our spiritual needs. So, in the Holy Place we can pause at the golden lampstands, the *menorhot*, and pray for more of the oil of his Spirit, and the gifts of his Spirit, in the lamps of our lives. And we can also pray for others. We can spend time daily at the golden altar of incense, bringing before the Father the names of those people, concerns and nations that are written upon our hearts.

Finally, in Chapter 6, we entered the Most Holy Place, the innermost sanctuary of God's Presence. Here we find the throne of God, where the High King of Heaven welcomes us with open arms. Now, in the throne zone as it were, the most important thing of all is to remember and to realise that the King is also a Father – the Father, in fact, whom we have been yearning for all our lives. Here, in the final stage of prayer, we express our love for the Father as we worship at his footstool. We sing, we sigh, we say the simple words, 'I love you, Dear Father.' There is no higher form of prayer than this. This is the purest kind of worship. As the devotional writer Richard Foster has said, 'worship is our response to the overtures of love from the heart of the Father'.

In the Secret Place of Prayer

In using the Temple model of prayer there are some simple guidelines of a general and practical nature that should be observed. The foundation for these is Jesus' teaching on prayer in Matthew 6:

> And now about prayer. When you pray, don't be like the hypocrites who love to pray publicly on street corners and in the synagogues where everyone can see them. I assure you, that is all the reward they will ever get. But when you pray, go away by yourself, shut the door behind you, and pray to your Father secretly. Then your Father, who knows all secrets, will reward you. When you pray, don't babble on and on as people of other religions do. They think their prayers are answered only by repeating their words again and again. Don't be like them, because your Father knows exactly what you need even before you ask him!

I draw five strategic life skills from this foundational teaching on prayer.

Life Skill 1: Decide on a regular time of prayer

Jesus starts by saying 'when you pray', not 'if you pray'. Jesus assumed that we would pray regularly. The onus of responsibility therefore rests on us to develop the spiritual discipline of prayer. This is part of the secret history of righteousness that is meant to characterise the normal Christian life. Along with financial giving and fasting (which are also mentioned in Matthew 6), prayer is one of those things that we make every effort to start and continue, from the time of our conversion onwards. This history is not to be public. In other words, we are not to indulge in the Pharisaical tendency of showing off by having our personal prayer time in the city centre, in full view of the general public, with the news cameras rolling, as it were. This is between us and God. It is an entirely private matter – we minister to an audience of one.

When is a good time for prayer? This is entirely a matter between you and the Father. As long as you give him some time in the day, I do not think for a moment that it really matters. Personally, I prefer to go through the stages of prayer described in this book before I begin the activities of what is invariably a very busy day. Spending time in the Father's presence enables me to enter into an inner place of rest. While things all around me may be loud and fast, deep within there will be a serenity that comes from having spent time in the presence of Jehovah Shalom, the Lord who is my Peace. So first thing in the morning is the optimum time for me personally, but I fully appreciate that other people prefer other times of the day.

How long should I pray for? Again, I do not think it really matters. When I preach or teach about personal prayer I no longer speak about the 'quiet time' but about 'quality time'. It is quality, not quantity, that counts. Three hours of religious platitudes cannot compare with three minutes of simple, heartfelt and utterly real worship.

Life Skill 2: Choose a quiet and private place

The secret of praying, as the saying goes, is praying in secret. Jonathan Edwards once made the point, in his marvellously entitled *Hypocrites Deficient in the Duty of Prayer* (1742), that the person who only prays when in the presence of others does not have a true and healthy respect for prayer at all. He is more concerned about the eyes of others than the all-seeing eye of God.

Jesus says, 'go away by yourself and shut the door behind you'. I love that detail, 'shut the door behind you'. Whatever place we choose, it needs to be somewhere where we are unlikely to experience interruptions and distractions. As we shut out the world with all its clamouring voices, we can focus more intensely upon the discipline and delight of prayer. As we shut the door and spend time with God, we are far more likely to encounter the light of his presence than if we try to pray on the move and in a crowded place (though this is not impossible either).

Someone once related to me the story of a preacher who was visiting the United States. He was walking the streets and found that he needed to make a phone call. He went into a telephone booth but found it was different from those in the UK. It was dark outside and he could not read the number he wanted from the directory. He could see that there was a light in the ceiling, but he could not find a switch anywhere. As he tried to find the number, a passer-by noticed his difficulty and said, 'If you want to turn the light on, you have to shut the door.' As the preacher shut the door, the light indeed came on. He was able to find the number and make the call.

If we want the light of God's presence, if we want to connect with the Father in prayer, then we need to choose a quiet and private place and close the door. Jesus called this our 'secret place'. The word in Greek is *tameion*, and it referred to the secret room in a Jewish home where the family treasure was hidden. Somewhere in our home we need to have a secret place where we enjoy the invaluable treasure of the Father's presence.

Life Skill 3: Focus on your Father in heaven

Jesus simply encourages us to 'pray to our Father'. I have mentioned this in the chapter on the Holy of Holies so I do not need to develop this too much now. It is just to remind us of the importance, as Christians, of having a truly trinitarian approach to prayer. True prayer is made to the Father, through Jesus (in his name), in the power of the Holy Spirit. Our prayer life should always be 'to the Father'. It should be directed ultimately to the perfect Father who is worthy of our worship. Jesus said that the Father is looking for worshippers (John 4:23). The word for 'worship' in this passage is *proskuneo* which means 'to approach someone in order to embrace them'. The Father is looking for those who will draw near to him and enjoy his affectionate embrace. He is not the kind of Father who is too busy to meet with us, or who resents spending time with us. Rather, he is the perfect Father who is always available, always faithful and always welcoming. We should focus on our Heavenly Father in prayer.

What this highlights more than anything else is that the most important thing about prayer is to have a proper focus on who you are praying to. I love what Anne Murchison says in this regard:

> I have read many books on prayer, studied prayer and attended seminars on prayer. I have prayed tens of thousands of hours privately and met with beloved friends over years and years to pray. I have attended church prayer meetings, prayed at church rallies, at community prayer meetings . . . I have prayed walking, standing, sitting, rocking babies. Kneeling and lying on my face. In all of this prayer over so many years I have learned one thing. One single thing . . . and this is that the power of prayer is not in the words I pray, the

place I pray, the way I pray, how loud I pray, or how long I pray, but in the One to Whom I pray.

Focus on the Father in prayer. That is where true power in prayer is to be found.

Life Skill 4: Be real, not religious, as you pray

Jesus tells us not to babble on (the original word is the onomato-poeic *battalogeo* in Greek) as we pray. Vain repetition is something people of other religions engage in. This is not for the Christian. When Christians pray, they are to be simple and sincere in the vocabulary they use. As we go through the stages of prayer described in this book, we do not need to use Shakespearean English or theological jargon. We need to speak to God in the same way we would speak to our spouse or our closest friend. As the saying goes, 'Our prayers must mean something to us if they are to mean something to God!'

Someone has pointed out that there are 800,000 words in the English language. Of these, 300,000 are technical terms. The average person knows 10,000 words and uses 5,000 in everyday conversation. When you pray, use language from the 5,000 words you use in ordinary conversational speech.

John Mason (1646–94) wrote: 'Prayer does not consist in the elegance of the phrase but in the strength of the affection.' I personally do not think there is any turn of phrase that we can use which will cause eyebrows to be raised in heaven and God to say, 'That's truly impressive; I haven't heard that expression before.' I do, however, believe that there is a way of praying that is born of an intensity of love, a distinctive and rare passion for God, that causes all of heaven to stop and the angels to hold their breath in wonder. It is the simple prayer of the heart that says with unadorned honesty and tearful feeling, 'I love you, Lord.' We need to keep it real.

Life Skill 5: Put relationship before requests

Jesus reminds us that our Father in heaven knows what our needs are before we even ask. So why bother asking at all? The truth is, prayer is primarily about relationship rather than requests. Requests are important and Jesus encourages us elsewhere on more than one occasion to ask. But the real priority is relationship.

The Father simply loves having us approach him, drawing near to him in prayer. He is much more interested in our company than our prayer list, though he has assured us he will hear us when we pray.

In prayer there is nothing we can tell God that will surprise him. But there is something we can do that will delight him – that is, spend time each day, in a secret place, telling him that we love him. The priority has to do with being rather than doing – being in the Father's presence, simply saying, 'I love you, Father.'

A very poor farmer got into the habit of entering a church at midday every day. There he would sit and apparently do nothing. The vicar noticed this silent visitor and one day was unable to restrain his curiosity any longer. 'Why are you doing this every day?' he asked. The old man looked at the vicar and explained, 'I come in here and he looks at me and I look at him. And we tell each other that we love each other.'

Practising the Presence of God

There is one more thing.

Spending quality time with the Father, ministering to him as a priest of the Kingdom, is something we set time aside to do. It requires discipline. Whether we set aside minutes or hours, we are still setting aside time. But this does not mean that we finish communicating with the Father the moment we finish our devotional time. I spend 10 to 15 minutes with my wife Alie every morning at our kitchen table, chatting and praying, before going our separate ways into the day. But that is not the last time in 24 hours that I communicate with her. We are constantly communicating, by telephone, email, further conversations, loving touches, and so forth. I do not say to Alie, 'You have had your 15 minutes.' We have our structured, set time but we also have further spontaneous times beyond that.

So it is with the Father. We have our set time – ministering to him using the Temple model of prayer – but thereafter we are constantly talking with him and listening to his voice. We encounter his presence in our set time, but we then practise and indeed carry the presence of God throughout the rest of the day, ministering the presence to those who do not know God.

Lesslie Newbigin has reminded us that 'The office of a priest is to stand before God on behalf of people and to stand before people on behalf of God.'[1] In other words, priesthood is not only about bringing people to God in prayer (the substance of this book). It is also about bringing something of the presence of God to where people are.

Thus our priesthood is not confined to the sacred parts of life; it is also to be exercised in what is called the secular realm. As Newbigin goes on to say:

> the exercise of this priesthood is not within the walls of the church but the daily business of the world. It is only in this way that the public life of the world, its accepted habits and assumptions, can be challenged by the gospel and brought under the searching light of the truth as it has been revealed in Jesus.[2]

In the final analysis, says Newbigin,

> it is the whole Church which is called to be – in Christ – a royal priesthood . . . every member of the body is called to the exercise of this priesthood, and . . . this priesthood is to be exercised in the daily life and work of Christians and in the secular business of the world.[3]

I agree with these sentiments entirely. Priesthood is not only about ministering *to* God in the secret and sacred place. It is also about ministering *for* God in the public and mundane place. That is why Paul speaks of the 'priestly duty of proclaiming the Gospel of God, so that the Gentiles might become an offering acceptable to God, sanctified by the Holy Spirit' (Romans 15:16). The words 'priestly duty' (*leiturgos*, from which we get 'liturgy') should strike a chord within us. This book has been a detailed description of priestly duties, duties which involve representing people before God. But here Paul talks about priestly duties in the context of representing God to people, of preaching the Gospel to the Gentiles.

Jimmy Dunn has pointed out that there is an intense concentration of Temple terminology in these verses: 'priestly duty', 'an offering acceptable to God', 'sanctified by the Holy Spirit'. By applying this language to the ministry of evangelism, Paul confirms that for him, the cultic barrier between sacred and secular has been broken through and left behind. And by speaking of the Gentiles as themselves the altar of sacrifice in the Temple . . . Paul confirms that for him the culturally defined barrier between peoples, between Jew and Gentile, has been broken through and left behind.[4]

For Paul, sharing the Gospel is the work of a priest (*hierourgeo*).

In the final analysis, the example of Paul is a strong argument against erecting an iron curtain between the sacred and the secular. Our priesthood is not to be a secret and sectarian ministry. It is to be a bold and open ministry of service in the world. We need to keep practising the presence of God beyond our set devotional time, and we need to carry the fire of the Father's love to those whom we meet every day.

So after all is said and done, we need to pray:

Send us out
in the power of your Spirit,
to live and work
to your praise and glory.
Amen.

Using the Temple Model in Corporate Worship

This book has really been designed for enriching one's *personal* prayer life through the use of Temple symbolism. However, this Temple model can also be used in acts of public worship. What follows is a breakdown of the event.

Preparation

Make sure you have the visuals of the layout and the furniture of the Temple on a service sheet, overhead projector slides, or best of all, PowerPoint. These visuals help people to see the act of worship as a gradual journey into the Holy of Holies.

Having prepared the visuals, the next thing to do is to create a worshipful ambience. Use dimmed lighting plus candles if appropriate. Particularly useful is a focal point. Place nightlights around the foot of the cross. Quiet music is appropriate as people come in, either from a worship group or over your sound system, using pre-recorded music.

Worship

Once people are settled and the music has stopped playing, the first stage is a matter of waiting on the Holy Spirit. Invite the Holy Spirit, either using your own words or a set prayer or song.

A period of thanksgiving and praise can be run together very effectively, using both ancient and modern hymns, and open declarations of worship from the floor. Spontaneity (being led by the Spirit) is very important at this point, as indeed it is all the way through. Encouraging people to reflect on God's blessings is the place to start; then you can move on to God's nature, encouraging people to praise the Lord for who he is.

In the confession, liturgy can be important. Silent reflection on where we stand with God can be followed by a set prayer, either from a liturgical service or from the Scriptures (e.g. Psalm 51).

It's quite powerful to move closer to the candle-lit altar at this point. People can either sit in the seats near the front or on cushions on the floor. At this stage we are moving from the outer court into the sanctuary.

There then follows a period of silence. In the silence, people are encouraged to listen to the promptings of the Spirit and to speak them out. Usually a common theme emerges in the pictures and words that are shared. This theme is then picked up by the person leading the prayers, who encourages us to intercede in response to the words. That way the congregation learns to discern the mind of Christ and to pray in the Spirit. Intercession is best made aloud, though those who want to think, sigh or pray inaudibly in tongues are encouraged to do so.

When the intercessions come to an end, the leader conducts a meditation on the throne of God in Revelation 4. This is best done as a voiceover: in other words, music in the background quietly (either live or pre-recorded), while the worship leader gets people focused on the Father enthroned in heaven. The melody should be one that can feed into a song like 'Holy, Holy, Holy' which focuses on the Father's throne. This climactic part of the service is best conducted with everyone standing, hands raised (if they are comfortable with that) to heaven.

After the meditation there is silence and resting in the presence of the Lord. The Grace then follows, with all joining hands and looking at each other.

Finally, appropriate music is played as people leave.

A Liturgy based on the Temple Model

The following was sent by a minister who has been using *A Kingdom of Priests* as the basis for corporate worship.

Introduction: The Jerusalem Temple.

+ In the Name of the Father, and of the Son, and of the Holy Spirit. **Amen.**

Invocation of the Holy Spirit
O Heavenly King, O Comforter, the Spirit of Truth, who is in all places and fills all things, the treasury of blessings, and giver of life, come and abide in us. Cleanse us from all impurity and save our souls, O gracious Lord.

Eastern Orthodox Church

1. *The Gate of Thanksgiving:* Thanking God
Enter his gates with thanksgiving and his courts with praise; give thanks to him and praise his name.

Psalm 100:4

This is the day that the Lord has made.
All: **Let us rejoice and be glad in it.**
Let us pray.

Almighty God, we thank you
for sending your holy and life-giving Spirit
to inspire all that is good in mankind,
to be the giver of life in the Church,
to help us grow in the likeness of Christ,
and to serve you as a holy people,
spreading your Gospel among all the nations.
Amen.

Hymn: 'I will enter His gates . . .'

2. *The Court of Praise:* Praising God
My soul yearns, even faints, for the courts of the Lord;
my heart and my flesh cry out for the living God.
Even the sparrow has found a home,
and the swallow a nest for herself,

where she may have her young – a place near your altar,
O Lord Almighty, my King and my God.

Psalm 84:2–4

Let us pray.

Almighty God,
help us to offer through Jesus Christ our High Priest,
a true sacrifice of praise.
We want to confess Jesus as Lord in the court of praise.
We want to celebrate the uniqueness of Jesus
in a world that has reduced him to just a man.
We pay homage to the Word made flesh,
true God and true man.

Hymn: 'Praise to the Lord, the Almighty, the King of creation' (MP 192).

3. *The Altar of Sacrifice:* Repentance

The Lord is full of compassion and great mercy,
slow to anger and of great kindness.
He has not dealt with us according to our sins,
nor rewarded us according to our wickedness.
For as the heavens are high above the earth,
So great is his mercy upon those who fear him.

Silence is kept.

(The *Trisagion hymn* is played on CD.)

Holy God, **Holy God!**
Holy Mighty, **Holy Mighty!**
Holy Immortal, **Holy Immortal!**
Have mercy on us, **have mercy on us.**
Glory to the Father, and to the Son, and to the Holy Spirit.
Both now and ever, and unto the ages of ages.
Amen.

As far as the East is from the West,
so far has he set our sins from us.
As a Father has compassion on his children,
so the Lord is merciful towards those who fear him.
Bless the Lord, O my soul,
and forget not his benefits.

Hymn: 'Dear Lord and Father of mankind . . .'

4. *The Altar of Incense:* Intercession

Let my prayer rise before you as incense,
the lifting up of my hands as the evening sacrifice.

Psalm 141

Refrain: **Preserve me, O God, for in you have I taken refuge.**

Psalm 61:
1. Hear my crying, O God,*
and listen to my prayer.
2. From the end of the earth
I will call to you with fainting heart,*
O set me on the rock that is higher than I.
3. For you are my refuge,*
a strong tower against the enemy.
4. Let me dwell in your tent forever*
and take refuge under the cover of your wings.
Preserve me, O God, for in you have I taken refuge.

5. For you, O God, will hear my vows;*
you will grant the request of those who fear your name.
6. You will add length of days to the life of the king,*
that his years may endure throughout all generations.
7. May he sit enthroned before God for ever;*
may steadfast love and truth watch over him.
8. So will I always sing praise to your name,*
and day by day fulfil my vows.
Preserve me, O God, for in you have I taken refuge.

O God, our rock and our refuge,
as Jesus knew the discipline of suffering
and the victory that brings us salvation,
so grant us his fellowship in our weakness
and a place in his unending Kingdom.

The Lord's Prayer
Standing at the foot of the cross,
let us pray with confidence as our Saviour has taught us.

Our Father, who art in heaven,
hallowed be thy name.
Thy kingdom come,
thy will be done,
in earth as it is in heaven.
Give us this day our daily bread.
And forgive us our trespasses,

as we forgive them that trespass against us.
And lead us not into temptation;
but deliver us from evil:
for thine is the kingdom,
the power, and the glory,
for ever and ever. Amen.

5. *The Most Holy Place:* Beholding the Throne
Around your throne in heaven angelic powers exalt you
with ceaseless hymns and unending songs of praise;
so may your praise be ever on our lips
that we may proclaim the greatness of your holy Name.

Praying with the Orthodox Tradition (SPCK, 1989)

Meditation
The Throne of God (Revelation 4): Heavenly Temple, Heavenly Worship.

After these things I looked, and behold, a door standing open in heaven . . .

Revelation 4:1

Hymn: 'Be still, for the presence of the Lord' (CD, 23 NH & WS).

The Divine Praises
Blessed be God.
Blessed be God.
Blessed be the Holy and undivided Trinity.
Blessed be the Holy and undivided Trinity.
Blessed be God the Father, maker of heaven and earth.
Blessed be God the Father, maker of heaven and earth.
Blessed be Jesus Christ, truly divine and truly human.
Blessed be Jesus Christ, truly divine and truly human.
Blessed be the holy name of Jesus.
Blessed be the holy name of Jesus.
Blessed be Jesus Christ in his death and resurrection.
Blessed be Jesus Christ in his death and resurrection.
Blessed be Jesus Christ on his throne of glory.
Blessed be Jesus Christ on his throne of glory.
Blessed be Jesus Christ in the sacrament of his body and blood.
Blessed be Jesus Christ in the sacrament of his body and blood.
Blessed be God the Holy Spirit, the giver and sustainer of life.
Blessed be God the Holy Spirit, the giver and sustainer of life.
Blessed be the Virgin Mary, Mother of God incarnate.
Blessed be the Virgin Mary, Mother of God incarnate.
Blessed be God in his angels and in his saints.
Blessed be God in his angels and in his saints.
Blessed be God.
Blessed be God.

Almighty and everlasting God,
who in your tender love towards the human race
sent your Son our Saviour Jesus Christ
to take upon him our flesh
and to suffer death upon the Cross:
grant that we may follow the example of his patience and humility,
and also be made partakers of his resurrection;
through Jesus Christ our Lord. **Amen.**

May Christ, who bore our sins on the Cross,
set us free to serve him with joy. **Amen.**

Let us bless the Lord.
Thanks be to God.

NOTES

Introduction

1. St Teresa of Avila, *The Interior Castle*, trans. by John Vernard (Sydney, 1988), pp. 26–7.
2. ibid., p. 1.

Chapter 1: Preparing for the Journey

1. Raniero Cantalamessa, *Come, Creator Spirit* (Minnesota, Liturgical Press, 2003), pp. 365–6.
2. John Donne, quoted in *1500 Illustrations for Preaching and Teaching*, compiled by Robert Backhouse (London, Marshall Pickering, 1991), p. 294.
3. R. Lovelace, *Dynamics of Spiritual Life* (Exeter, Paternoster Press, 1979), p. 155.
4. A. Murray, *The Prayer Life* (London, Marshall, Morgan & Scott, 1968), p. 53.
5. T. S. Eliot, *The Use of Poetry and the Use of Criticism* (London, Faber, 1975), p. 146.
6. See C. Di Sante, *Jewish Prayer* (New York, Paulist Press, 1985), p. viii.
7. Richard Rolle, *The Fire of Love* (London, Penguin Classics, 1972), p. 93.
8. A new translation from *Religiøse Følelser og deres Værd* (Skrifter VI, 126.20–127.22) by Alie Stibbe.
9. Charles Finney, from the *Autobiography of Charles Finney*, published at the following website: www.matthew548.com/Finney3.html
10. J. Rodman Williams, published at the following website: home.regent.edu/rodmwil/tppre.html

Chapter 2: The Gates of Thanksgiving

1. Di Sante, *Jewish Prayer*, p. 104.
2. Charles L. Brown, *Content: The Newsletter*, June 1990, p. 3.
3. Murray, *The Prayer Life*, p. 54.
4. Di Sante, op. cit., p. 38.
5. S. T. Coleridge (13 July 1834, 12 days before his death). Cited in L. Weatherhead, *A Private House of Prayer* (London, Hodder & Stoughton, 1966), p. 217.
6. Mark Stibbe, *From Orphans to Heirs: Celebrating our Spiritual Adoption* (Oxford, Bible Reading Fellowship, 1995).

Chapter 3: The Court of Praise

1. St Teresa of Avila, *The Interior Castle*, p. 7.
2. M. Borg, *Jesus. A New Vision* (San Francisco, Harper & Row, 1987), p. 1.